THE CREATION
OF NEW IDEAS IN
PSYCHOTHERAPY

THE CREATION OF NEW IDEAS IN PSYCHOTHERAPY

A guidebook

ALVIN R MAHRER

PCCS Books

Ross-on-Wye

First published in 2006

PCCS BOOKS Ltd
2 Cropper Row
Alton Road
Ross-on-Wye
Herefordshire
HR9 5LA
UK
Tel +44 (0)1989 763 900
contact@pccs-books.co.uk
www.pccs-books.co.uk

**The Creation of New Ideas in Psychotherapy:
A guidebook**

British Library Cataloguing in Publication Data
A catalogue record for this book is available from the British Library

ISBN 1 898059 77 2
ISBN 978 1898059 77 6

Cover design by Old Dog Graphics

Printed by Bell & Bain, Glasgow, UK

CONTENTS

PREFACE

I graduated with a doctorate in 1954 and was quite sure at that point that I did not know how to do psychotherapy. It took many years for me to find a way of thinking about and cobbling together a way of doing psychotherapy that seemed to fit me and that I could do reasonably well. During all those years, most of my efforts were fairly practical, down to earth, learning, trial and error, studying, trying things out, on-the-job training. It seemed to be workmanlike slow progress rather than anything in the neighborhood of creativity. But I finally found a way for me to do psychotherapy at a point where many psychotherapists close their offices and find ways of enjoying life after psychotherapy.

Somehow, I am not sure how or why, that was just about the point where I turned to the neighboring field of philosophy of science, as a 'mature student', with a passion to find what philosophy of science had to say about how to come up with creative new ideas.

Why was I so enthusiastic about guidelines for coming up with creative new ideas?

Having spent so many years trying to figure out a way to make sense of what people are like and how this thing called 'psychotherapy' can work, I found myself facing some serious issues in the field of psychotherapy, issues that seemed deep, foundational, important, with powerful implications for the field.

I was facing, and overwhelmed by, issues about why we did psychotherapy research, what psychotherapy was for, what we took for granted as real and to be trusted, how we arrived at and adopted new foundational beliefs, how and why we had such different mind-sets in the field of psychotherapy, what we meant by 'personality' and what its origins were, what seemed to constitute this 'inner deeper world' that we talked about, what human beings could become, how our field could become more of what our field could become.

I felt like Don Quixote, tilting at windmills, unprepared and unable to do more than be impressed and overwhelmed by these deep and serious issues. Maybe philosophy of science could help. Philosophers of science knew about how to come up with creative new ideas. They knew about guidelines and principles that were beyond me.

The more I read and studied what philosophy of science had to say about guidelines for coming up with new ideas, the more passionate and enthusiastic I became about trying to understand and to make sense of these guidelines. This volume is my attempt to put these guidelines together and to offer them to interested psychotherapists, be they students, teachers, theorists, researchers or practitioners.

The guidelines in this volume are genuine guidelines, working tools that are to be used, rather than general discussion of creative new ideas. Although the premium is on applicability and usefulness, some of the guidelines are relatively simple and easy and some are difficult. Some are probably quite familiar and some much less so.

Over the course of years, when I was reading about and then writing about the guidelines, I was fortunate to be able to talk with philosophers of science who wrote about these topics. My main concern was not especially with how to use their principles and guidelines, but rather with their suggestions for what to study, and whether I seemed to come close to grasping what these philosophers of science were saying about how to come up with creative new ideas, about the actual guidelines. Talking with these people was so important.

My concern now is how to put these guidelines to use in better and better ways, how to extend them, modify them, improve them. If you are interested in these guidelines, I look forward to hearing from you. If you try out some of these guidelines, I would like to hear from you. If you have some interest in improving these guidelines, I would value hearing from you. My mailing address is Alvin R Mahrer, PhD, School of Psychology, University of Ottawa, Ottawa KIN 6N5, Canada. My email address is amahrer@uottawa.ca.

Finally, an invitation is personally extended to those rare souls, in or near the broad field of psychotherapy, who can put these guidelines to energetic and constructive work. These guidelines are for you. The invitation is for you to use these guidelines to enter into the world of creative new ideas, and to discover the creative new ideas that can advance the field of psychotherapy, that can revolutionize the field of psychotherapy theory, research, practice and training. Those guidelines call out to you, and the invitation is to put the guidelines to exciting, wonderful and marvelous use.

INTRODUCTION

Ways of Coming up with Creative New Ideas in the Field of Psychotherapy

Picture a psychotherapist who is mainly a theorist, a researcher, a practitioner, a teacher or supervisor, an administrator or member of staff, a student or trainee. Picture a psychotherapist with a great deal of experience or just starting out. Picture a psychotherapist who works mainly in a university or a clinic, in private practice or as a consultant. Or picture the field of psychotherapy as a whole.

In any case, here are the questions. How can we come up with creative new ideas? How can we stretch the limits, extend the outer boundaries of what we know? How can we open up and explore whole new territory, find and solve the secrets of psychotherapy, extend what is now taken for granted? How can we achieve wholesale paradigm-shifts? All of these are variations and extensions of the guiding question: what are some ways to come up with creative new ideas in the field of psychotherapy?

1. The purpose is to talk with psychotherapists who are ready to have creative new ideas

During training programs in psychotherapy, it is not especially common to talk about having creative new ideas, about students' readiness to have creative new ideas. Having creative new ideas is not an especially common topic of discussion. It is not much of a topic in courses or in field work, internships and residencies. In general, students are to learn what the profession has to teach. Having creative new ideas may float here and there in most training programs, but it is not an especially recognized topic of special interest and study.

The purpose of this volume is to talk with the teachers and the staff, the students and the trainees, of these training programs. Are any of you truly interested in having creative new ideas? I expect that very few teachers and students would have a genuine glow of interest, but even very few is enough. My purpose is to talk with those teachers and students who are truly interested in having creative new ideas.

I also want to make contact with the psychotherapists who make up the profession, with the practitioners and the researchers and the theoreticians and those who hold the various administrative positions. Of all these people, the aim is especially to talk with those who have even a spark of readiness to have creative new ideas.

Some psychotherapists have a track record of thinking about and coming up with creative new ideas. Most psychotherapists do not. The purpose is to talk with all of these people in the hope that some may well be ready to think about, to consider, to have creative new ideas.

2. The purpose is to suggest some useful guidelines to help you to come up with creative new ideas

One way of thinking (e.g. Gardner, 1993) is that truly creative new ideas come from truly creative people, rare and special people with a remarkable quality of 'creative brilliance'. The field of psychotherapy benefited from the creative genius of such rare souls as Sigmund Freud, HS Sullivan, Carl Rogers, DW Winnicott, William James, Abraham Maslow, BF Skinner, Carl Jung, Clark Hull, Milton Erickson, and others in or near the field of psychotherapy.

In this way of thinking, truly creative new ideas are unlikely to spring from the minds of ordinary psychotherapists, be they theoreticians, researchers, practitioners or teachers. Even if we could come up with a list of guidelines, it would be a waste of time, a fruitless quest, perhaps a cruel thing to do, to think that the great preponderance of ordinary psychotherapists would be able to use the useful guidelines. Psychotherapeutic theoreticians, researchers, practitioners and teachers would hardly acknowledge such a list, and even less probably use the guidelines to come up with creative new ideas. That requires the rare psychotherapist with creative brilliance and genius.

What is more, in this way of thinking, there are no useful guidelines, no useful principles or methods, to generate creative new ideas, at least in this broad and extended field of psychotherapy.

> There is no such thing as a logical method of having new ideas, or a logical reconstruction of the process. My view may be expressed by saying that every discovery contains an 'irrational element,' or a 'creative intuition,' in Bergson's sense. (Popper, 1980: 32; cf. Gadamer, 1975; Weinsheimer, 1985)

Don't even bother looking for useful principles. There are none to be found.

There is an alternative way of thinking in which it is possible to identify some useful guidelines, working principles, for coming up with creative new ideas in the field of psychotherapy. This is the way of thinking underlying the work of some philosophers of science, theoreticians and researchers who have studied how creative new ideas have come about in a fair number of fields (e.g. Amabile, 1983; Barron, 1969; Csikszentmihalyi, 1997; Gedo, 1997; Glover, Ronning and Reynolds, 1989; Guilford, 1950; Simonton, 2000; Tyler, 1983). I value their way of thinking because it helped to lead me to search for some useful guidelines, and I value their work because it helped me to clarify some of the useful guidelines.

The more I read the works of philosophers of science, the more impressed I was with their study of the history of creative new ideas in other sciences. It was like reading captivating stories about how these ideas were conceived and born. It was also captivating because philosophers of science brought a way of thinking that seemed to include actual principles these creative scientists followed in coming up with their creative ideas.

It seemed to me that these philosophers of science talked very little about the creative giants in the field of psychotherapy theory, research and practice. Indeed, these philosophers of science seemed to talk very little about the field of psychotherapy. Perhaps the main credit I can give myself is being puzzled by what seemed to be some nagging questions. Philosophers of science seemed to know about what might be called principles for coming up with creative new ideas in the sciences they studied. Could these principles be applied to the field of psychotherapy? Could our theorists, researchers and practitioners follow these principles and use them to come up with creative new ideas? What were these principles? If they could be understood and put into simple words, could they be applied to help the field of psychotherapy to come up with creative new ideas?

Accordingly, the purpose of this volume is to turn to philosophy of science in order to identify some principles that could be used in the field of

3

psychotherapy to help people to come up with creative new ideas. To a large extent, the underlying principles are from the way of thinking found in the work of many philosophers of science.

In line with their way of thinking, the purpose is to suggest some working guidelines for coming up with creative new ideas. By 'working' I mean that the guidelines are concrete and doable. They can be learned. They can be followed. They are working guidelines rather than abstract principles that are hard to follow, abstract principles such as 'Set aside your basic assumptions and receive the phenomenon in order to enter the realm of creative ideas', or 'The context for creative ideas is a state of passive receptivity', or 'Creativity is a matter of innovative thinking'. In contrast, the purpose is to provide some working guidelines that can be relatively simple, concrete, doable.

Furthermore, the purpose is to provide working guidelines that can be followed by psychotherapy practitioners and theoreticians and researchers. They can be followed by psychotherapists who hold to a psychodynamic approach or a cognitive behavioral approach or an integrative approach or just about any other approach. They can be followed by psychotherapists who are seasoned and experienced or by psychotherapists with little experience in the field. They can be followed by teachers and by students in the field of psychotherapy.

2.1 Some of the proposed guidelines are easy, and some can be difficult

Some of the guidelines are easy. They can fit with what you already believe, do not require a significant shift in your foundational ideas about psychotherapy. They have a certain tone of familiarity, rather than coming across as weird or alien. Nor do they require substantial training to acquire the requisite skills. It is more a matter of getting the general idea and then going ahead and coming up with creative new ideas. They are kinds of guidelines you might expect to get from a good workshop or training seminar on guidelines for creative new ideas.

On the other hand, some of the guidelines can be quite difficult, can call for quite a bit of work. (a) Some of the guidelines can work if you adopt a particular way of thinking. If your mind-set can accommodate that altered way of thinking, you have a good chance of carrying out the guideline. However, if the guideline is tied to a particular way of thinking, and if that way of thinking is too alien, too risky, too threatening, then that particular guideline is not especially ready for you, and you are not especially ready for that particular guideline. (b) Some of the guidelines involve skills that call for substantial training, proficiency. Learning the skills can be more than merely getting the idea from a workshop, or rehearsing the skill a few times with a co-learner.

It seems to be that some of the guidelines are relatively easy and some can be rather difficult. Expect both kinds of guidelines for creative new ideas.

3. The purpose is to suggest some useful guidelines for psychotherapists with a passion for creative new ideas

Here is the question: are you passionately enthusiastic about creative new ideas, about receiving and coming up with creative new ideas that can help revolutionize the field of psychotherapy practice, theory, research, education and training?

This glow of passionate enthusiasm is perhaps the singular prerequisite for being able to come up with creative new ideas in this field. You may have this special quality whether or not you have had a track record of creative new ideas, whether you are just beginning or have had some experience in the field, whether you are primarily a practitioner or a theorist, a researcher or a teacher, a student or an administrator.

Here is the test. As you read more and more about what is meant by creative new ideas, and perhaps as you read about a few of the guidelines, is there a coming to life of some genuine interest? This 'passion' may already be alive and well in you, and of moderate size. Or there may be a tiny flickering glow of passion that may turn on and off as you read. In any case, you are the person to whom this volume is hoping to talk.

3.1 Is this passion relatively common or relatively rare?
My impression is that even a gleam of this passion is relatively rare in the field of psychotherapy. If a teacher or a visiting speaker were to address a hundred or so students and trainees, to discuss creative new ideas, and to invite a decision to make a small commitment to engaging in the learning of the guidelines, my impression is that only a token few might actually take up the invitation. My impression is that only a tiny proportion of students and trainees can show some evidence of a passion for creative new ideas.

My impression is that most students would essentially decline. 'I am a little interested, but I am busy right now. Maybe later.' 'I am not all that interested. There are other things on my mind.' 'I don't know what you are talking about. The whole field of scientific psychology deals with creative new ideas all the time.' 'I have some questions about this notion of creative new ideas.' 'Most of my training has to do with new ideas, so I'm not sure what the problem is.' 'You want an honest answer? I am enthusiastic about psychotherapy theory and research and practice, but not much in my trying to come up with big new creative ideas, not really.' 'Show me some creative new ideas, and I'll tell you what I think about them.' 'There's an area in psychology about creativity. It's not my particular specialty, no.' 'I would like to hear some of your guidelines so I can check them out.' 'I am passionate about the science of psychology, not about trying to speculate.'

My impression is much the same for the field as a whole. Thankfully, there are some psychotherapists who do have this passion for creative new ideas. They may publish or may not. They may read or they may not. They may be practitioners or researchers or theorists or teachers. However, with these rare exceptions, my impression is that a glow of passion for new ideas is essentially a missing commodity in the field of psychotherapy.

If my impression is wrong, I am glad. If my impression is accurate, I am sad. It would be so gratifying to see almost any evidence that there is a substantial stirring of a passion for creative new ideas. It almost doesn't seem to matter whether this is evidence of a shift, from little or no passion to the growth of some genuine passion, or whether this is evidence of the continued presence of a fair degree of this passion in the field. However, in the meantime, my impression is that a passion for creative new ideas is a rare and lonely quality, wandering around the large and alien field of psychotherapy.

In any case, this volume is trying to find and talk with those psychotherapists with even a tiny flickering glow of passion for creative new ideas. The glow may be faint or radiant, and the glow may be inside many psychotherapists or exceedingly few. It is the talking together that can be important.

3.2 Some creative new ideas can be relatively safe, and some can be exceedingly threatening

Some creative new ideas can be friendly, even welcomed and appealing. They can be seen as clever, as innovations, as advances, as new developments, as creative new ideas. They are seen as helpful further extensions of what we know and do, as helpful implications, as helpful broader generalizations, as new and better ways of grasping and understanding, as new and better ways of doing what we do. We like these creative new ideas. They are friendly, safe, helpful.

There can be at least two reasons why some creative new ideas are relatively safe, even welcomed:

(a) We can like these creative new ideas because they are friendly to our basic truths, our foundational beliefs, our canons and dictums, our anchoring cornerstones, what we take for granted as fundamental and basic and true. The creative ideas fit. We don't have to think about it. We just know that the creative ideas fit.

(b) We can like these creative ideas because they are friendly to what we do. They accept what we accept about what psychotherapy is for, the reasons and purposes for the field, the mission and aims of the noble field of psychotherapy. Indeed, these creative ideas are friendly because they can carry the field forward. They can advance the field, make it better. They can even enhance the mission and aims of psychotherapy, refine and extend them, make them better, bigger, bolder. What we do is advanced because of these creative new ideas.

On the other hand, the other sides of these same two reasons can be reasons why some creative new ideas are seen as exceedingly threatening:

(a) The creative new idea is sensed as fatal to our *basic truths*, as violating our *foundational beliefs*, as destroying our *canons and dictums*, as shattering the very cornerstones of what we take for granted as basic and true. We can sense that these dreadful new ideas mean we must abandon, lose, give up virtually everything we had taken for granted. These dreadful new ideas signal their death, the end of the existence of our basic beliefs. We may not know exactly what these fundamental givens are, we may not be able to call them up and spell them out, but when we are face to face with some creative new ideas, we can react to them as exceedingly dangerous and threatening, even though we may not be able to be clear about how and why they are so exceedingly dangerous and threatening.

(b) The creative new idea violates and shatters virtually everything we take for granted as the *mission and aims* of psychotherapy. The creative new idea kills what we do as psychotherapists and the aims and goals of doing what we do. Psychotherapy itself is wrenched out of shape, is extinguished, ended, gone, no longer exists.

This destruction is not confined to particular therapies and approaches, nor does it favor rival therapies and approaches. Rather, what is likely is wholesale destruction of virtually everything that is common to the field of psychotherapy, including the mission and goals common to most therapies and approaches. The creative new idea is a monstrous threat to psychotherapy as helping people with their psychological problems, reducing symptoms, dealing with 'presenting complaints', treating mental disorders. The new idea menaces the therapist–client relationship, who and what psychotherapy is for, the very roles of 'therapist' and 'client,' what psychotherapy is to achieve, how to achieve what psychotherapy can achieve, the place of psychotherapy in the lives of people.

When the creative new idea is menacing and threatening, dangerous and scary, it is no longer a creative new idea. It is something menacing and threatening, dangerous and scary, and it is dealt with as the bothersome thing that it is. When the idea is friendly and safe, it may live and be as a creative new idea. When the idea is unfriendly and threatening, it is an unfriendly and threatening idea, not a creative new idea.

This volume is not trying to sell any particular kinds of creative new ideas. It does not favor one creative idea over another. This volume is trying to persuade interested psychotherapists to try out some guidelines or principles to help them in coming up with creative ideas, and this includes all sorts of creative new ideas, regardless of their content. This may not be much of a problem when the creative idea is relatively friendly and safe. On the other hand, this can be a serious problem when the searcher is coming into the vicinity of a creative idea that is unfriendly and threatening to the one who is searching. The serious problem can become much more conspicuous when a creative idea is identified and offered in good faith to psychotherapists who are galvanized into shutting tight against and attacking an idea that is sensed as unfriendly, threatening, menacing, dangerous.

3.3 A heartfelt appeal to psychotherapists with the relatively common inclination to shut tight against and to attack creative new ideas that are threatening

I believe it is exceedingly common to sense how exceedingly threatening some creative new ideas can be, and then to react in one or both of two ways. One way is to shut tight against these creative ideas. It is as if something inside says, 'I don't want to know about these ideas. I don't want to see them, hear about them. I don't know exactly what they are, and I do not want to know. I will dance away, push them away, close up against them, go numb, shut down, change the subject, do anything to avoid them, distance them, make them go away.'

Shutting tight against a threatening creative new idea can include seeing or hearing something other than the threatening creative idea. In all honesty, and without malice or bad feeling, the person sees and hears something altogether different. Instead of seeing or hearing the creative new idea, the person has converted it into a benign different notion, into a friendly different idea, into something altogether different from what it is. Or the person converts it into a qualitatively different idea that is rather bizarre, silly, wild, far fetched, and utterly different from what it really is. The person has wholly distorted the creative idea into being something other than the creative idea that it is.

Another way is to attack the creative idea or the person who is developing and fostering the creative idea. Show that the creative idea is not a creative idea. We already know that idea. That creative idea falls under this larger category, and we are already familiar with this larger category. The creative idea is illogical, makes little sense, is not supported by research, violates what we know is true. Attack the person with the creative idea. She lacks proper knowledge. Be suspicious of her motivation for developing the creative idea. Trivialize her idea, marginalize her and her idea, refuse to publish her creative idea. Force her to recant, to accept our truths rather than cling to her creative idea. Pressure her to voice our truths. Show how she has inadequate evidence, is marginal, is not one of us. Show how her creative idea is like that other creative idea which proved to be a poor idea. Accuse her of being offensive, antagonistic, not presenting her creative idea in a way of which we approve.

What follows is a twofold appeal to those with the relatively common inclination to shut tight against or to attack creative new ideas or even the idea of guidelines for being able to come up with creative new ideas. The twofold appeal is heartfelt but rather faint because I have serious doubts whether either of them can be even mildly successful. Nevertheless, here are the two appeals:

(a) Please use your reactions as indications that there may be something of value in the creative new ideas or the idea of guidelines for coming up with creative new ideas. It is understandable that you react by shutting tight or by attacking. Perhaps these reactions to threat mean you can set aside or go beyond the threat. See whether there might be something of real worth and value in whatever threatens you. Can you please consider this possibility?

(b) Please be tolerant of those who are drawn toward knowing about and following some guidelines for coming up with creative new ideas. Let these people be. Try to be willing to allow interested others to have a little room for their trying to pursue creative new ideas. Hold back your inclination to shut down against these people or perhaps to attack them. Even if you have good and proper reasons for not joining them, or even to discount and object to what they are trying to accomplish, try to temper your inclinations enough to let them do what they want to do. Please be ready to see that what they are trying to do does not necessarily harm you, so you need not harm them. Please try to grant them the right to pursue creative new ideas even though you do not share their enthusiasm, even though you expect little or nothing of worth to come from their pursuit.

3.4 Have I used the guidelines and come up with creative new ideas?

When I work on this book, when I read the manuscript, I hear a voice inside. When I talk about ways of coming up with creative new ideas, I hear much the same voice, but it is usually coming from outside. In its more politely aggressive form, the voice says, 'If you know so much about creative new ideas, where are your own creative new ideas?' In its more confrontational form, the voice says, 'If these guidelines are so good, how come they don't work for you?' When I try to give voice to my own version of the voice, the voice says, 'Have I used the guidelines and been able to come up with creative new ideas?' I have three answers:

First, I can study, I can know about, I can appreciate and I can teach the guidelines for coming up with creative new ideas without my being an exemplary producer of creative new ideas. I can be a scholar of musical compositions without my necessarily being a great composer myself. A fine trainer can produce a fine boxer even though the trainer may not be a fine boxer himself. A fine scientist can arrive at a creative grasp of how these tiny fish reproduce, even though the scientist doesn't engage in reproduction with the tiny fish. I can show you how to have creative new ideas, even though I have no track record of creative new ideas.

'Have I used the guidelines and been able to come up with creative new ideas?' The question almost suggests that when I did my work, I knew about and I used the guidelines for coming up with creative new ideas. But this was not quite the case. For decades until fairly recently, my work was mainly trying to fashion some way for me to understand myself and others (Mahrer, 1989), to do psychotherapy in a way that made sense to me (Mahrer, 1996/2004, 2004c), to build a way of having an experiential session by and with oneself (Mahrer, 2002b), and to be able to do psychotherapy research to discover the secrets of psychotherapy (Mahrer, 1985, 1988, 1996a, 2004a; Mahrer and Boulet, 1999).

During those decades, I had little or no idea of guidelines for coming up with new ideas. Studying what philosophers of science had to say about creative new ideas came largely after I had spent four or five decades doing what I was doing. Most of my work does not qualify as a test to see whether the guidelines had a payoff or not.

The first two answers dodge the bullet. Here is a version of the bullet that is harder to dodge: 'Recently I have come to appreciate what philosophers of science have to say about ways of coming up with new ideas. Have I tried them out? Have I found that I can use them and come up with some creative new ideas?'

Here is a 'yes' answer. Now that I have some idea of ways to help people to come up with creative new ideas, when I read works on psychotherapy theory, practice, research and training, there are times when I can actually study a given paragraph or so, try to use a guideline, and my pleasantly surprised reaction is: 'I do believe this is a creative new idea, at least for me!' My track record may not be especially impressive, and I may not be especially skilled at using the guidelines, but I am able to study a particular passage, apply the guidelines as well as I can, and emerge with an idea that does strike me as new, for me, as having some interesting implications for the field of psychotherapy, and even as being at least somewhat creative, as far as I am concerned. Whether I am reading a given passage, or discussing something with others, or explicitly trying to apply a particular guideline, I have at least been able to come face to face with what seems to me to be a creative new idea. The answer is yes

Can I present you with some documented evidence of what I believe are the fruits of coming up with creative new ideas? Can I show you some creative new ideas that I have been able to come up with by using the helpful guidelines?

About a decade or so ago, I came to appreciate some of the guidelines for coming up with creative new ideas. Before that, I had plenty of work to do in trying to develop my own way of making sense of psychotherapy theory, research and practice. Once I turned to philosophy of science in a serious way, and came to grasp what seemed to be guidelines for coming up with creative new ideas, my work seemed to take a new direction. The focus seemed to become broader and deeper, to deal with issues having to do with the field as a whole.

By allowing these creative guidelines to guide my work, I found myself writing about matters far beyond what I had been working on. I found myself thinking and writing about the underlying serious problems whose solution might possibly revolutionize the field of psychotherapy research; about the possibly revolutionary implications of the field shifting from what might be called 'theories of truth' to 'models of usefulness'; about the powerful implications of extending the field to what might be called an 'optimal state'; about extending the field of psychotherapy supervision to include discovery of trainees' own 'deeper frameworks'; about alternative ways of making sense of the origins of personality; about how philosophy of science can suggest ways for the field of psychotherapy to become more of a science of psychotherapy; about the possibilities of picturing a qualitatively different, other, deeper, inner world; about how the nature, content, and existence of psychological things can be relative to the location of the 'knower'; and even about the interesting or exciting implications of borrowing and using what philosophy of science has to offer in regard to ways of coming up with creative new ideas.

Now I can answer the question directly: can I present you with some documented evidence of what I believe are the fruits of trying to apply these guidelines for coming up with creative ideas? I can show you a few books that came from my own attempts to put these guidelines into use. One is titled, *Theories of Truth, Models of Usefulness: Toward a revolution in the field of psychotherapy* (Mahrer, 2004b). Another is titled, *Why Do Research in Psychotherapy? An introduction to a revolution* (Mahrer, 2004a). A third is titled, *Supervision of Psychotherapists: The discovery-oriented approach* (Mahrer, 2005). I am completing works on each of the topics mentioned above.

These three books, and the works to follow, are my attempts to apply the creative guidelines, to put them to use in my own work. This is the documented evidence I can submit. Judge for yourself.

You may judge that the books offer at least some evidence that the creative guidelines have some promise. Or you may judge that the works are much ado about nothing, wasted energetic tiltings at windmills, the harmless activities of a senile psychologist, documented evidence that the creative guidelines have little or no future as creative guidelines.

Or you can judge that the creative guidelines can be useful, in and of themselves, quite aside from my personal and feeble attempts to put them to use in my own work. My personal hope is that you can and will put these creative guidelines to use in your own quest for creative new ideas in your own particular part of the field of psychotherapy.

4. How is the rest of the volume organized?

There are eight chapters, each dealing with its own general guideline for how to come up with creative new ideas in the field of psychotherapy, and this can include psychotherapy theory or practice, or research or education and training. Within each chapter are more specific guidelines under the general guideline.

Chapter 1 deals with a readiness to have creative new ideas. There seem to be qualities that go with this readiness, but, whether readiness is somewhat low or high, it is helpful to gain some working competency in the actual skills of creating new ideas.

Chapter 2 suggests how creative new ideas can be fostered and generated if you are inclined to be inside or outside the mainstream of the field of psychotherapy.

Chapter 3 deals with guidelines for coming up with creative new ideas by adopting a creative new perspective on the field of psychotherapy.

Chapter 4 shows how to use 'bodily-felt sensations' as tracking guides for coming up with creative new ideas.

Chapter 5 proposes guidelines for how to study a problem in order to come up with creative new ideas.

Chapter 6 offers some explicit guidelines for how to start with an idea and develop it into a creative new idea.

Chapter 7 provides guidelines for how a person can become more open to welcoming, having, being a wellspring of creative new ideas.

Chapter 8 consists of guidelines for entering into a 'creative relationship' with the thing, the issue, the subject matter that the person is studying.

CHAPTER 1

It Helps if You are Ready to Have Creative New Ideas

It is so important that you have that rare and special quality of a passionate enthusiasm for creative new ideas. But often this golden quality is buried inside a person who is ready or not especially ready to come up with creative new ideas. It helps if you are the kind of person who is truly ready to come up with creative new ideas. It also helps if you have the skills and competencies that enable you to be genuinely able to come up with creative new ideas.

1. It helps if you are a person with a big 'attitude problem'

Those who study creative people have some ideas of what creative people are like. For example,

> such persons are disposed to be independent, nonconformist, unconventional, even bohemian, and they are likely to have wide interests, greater openness to new experiences, a more conspicuous behavioral and cognitive flexibility, and more risk-taking boldness. (Simonton, 2000: 153)

These people have a passion for their work, a 'rage to master' (Csikszentmihalyi, 1997; Winner, 1996, 2000).

I would like to start with this kind of published version of what creative people in general are found to be like, and to personalize the description from talking with people who have been close to some creative people in the field of psychotherapy, from my own knowing of a few of these creative people in psychotherapy and from knowing some special students who seem to have this creative glow.

My impression is that these creative psychotherapy theorists and teachers and practitioners and researchers do seem to have some special qualities and characteristics. In other words, if you are even a little inclined to come up with creative new ideas in this field, my impression is that it helps if you have some particular kinds of personal qualities and characteristics, or if you can bring them to the surface, or if you can call upon these personal qualities and characteristics. Indeed, it seems that the more of these qualities you have, the better. The more deeply and intensely you have these qualities, the better.

As a package, the following qualities and characteristics may be seen in a positive way, as perhaps rosy and good. However, they can also be recognized as problematic, offensive, nasty, unappealing, not the qualities and characteristics you would expect in the saintly person or even in a person you might care to live with or work with or have dealings with. In other words, if you are inclined to come up with creative new ideas, it helps if you are a person with a big 'attitude problem'.

Here are some of these qualities and characteristics. If you are fortunate enough to have them, use them. Celebrate them and put them to work because they can help you to be ready to come up with creative new ideas.

1.1 You have a healthy disrespect for most of psychotherapy theory, research, practice and training

You come equipped with a built-in disrespect for most of the field, a critical attitude that refuses to swallow what most of the field cheerfully swallows. You have trouble singing the party line. If the authorities say it is true, you have serious doubts. If your supervisor says that this is the way to do psychotherapy, you cannot accept what she says. If your teacher says that this is the way to do psychotherapy research, you figure that is probably not true. If you are told that here are the common ingredients of successful psychotherapy, you cannot buy that.

If the field holds something as dear, precious, basic, foundational, true, your eyebrow rises, your eyes narrow, your jaw tightens, and your back gets up. If authorities agree, they are probably wrong. If most psychotherapists accept it as true, it is probably false.

You have a high-grade, deeply ingrained stubborn streak, and nothing can convince you that you are wrong. You are negative, rebellious and rigid. You have an authority problem. You have a big attitude problem. When 'they' shift the power tactics to explanations of what must be wrong with you because of your 'attitude problem', you reverse the tactic by turning to explanations of what must be wrong with them because of their having a serious problem of being bland unthinking sheep.

You have little or no respect for the cumulative body of research-generated knowledge. If they tell you that research confirms it or that research shows it, you steel up as if they are brainwashing you, forcing you to accept whatever it is. You have a healthy suspicion of pressure tactics gift-wrapped in authoritative research papers.

You know that you are being fed a cumulative body of research-approved knowledge, forced to recite the research-approved catechism, and that you must know what you are told to know or there can be severe penalties. You may well fail the course, be asked to leave the program, not finish the internship or residency, not pass the examination, not be accredited and licensed, not get the job. The penalties are serious, come in waves, and are hard-hitting. They are the penalties of your big attitude problem.

The field tells you that we know a great deal, we have a cumulative body of knowledge. We know enough to train professionals, to judge your knowledge, to assess your competency. It takes years to provide you with the knowledge that the field has accumulated, and even after you graduate it is important that you engage in continuing education to keep up with the expanding knowledge.

Your attitude problem says that we have barely scratched the surface of what there is to be known. We are primitive. We are ignorant. There are vast territories of knowledge we hardly know exist, and we have yet to explore these unknown territories. There is so much to be learned, so very much to be discovered.

The authoritative field is run by authoritative theories. You are to respect and to adopt the authoritative theories. However, your attitude problem knows that the authoritative theories are paper-thin, are filled with pompous gas, are dressed in fake authoritative robes, and can be created as easily and effortlessly as a popcorn popper pops popcorn. You know that almost any position you can hold can be justified and explained by some authoritative theory. You know that theories are silly and disposable even if they have been around for many years, are solemnly sanctioned by the grand authorities, are bolstered by hundreds of friendly scientific studies, and especially if they are swallowed by the masses.

Where the field celebrates its dominant theories, your big attitude problem says that we have yet to develop better and better theories, we have yet to truly grasp what theories are, we have yet to gain the knowledge for truly grand future theories.

17

> It is as if the discipline is content to believe that all the possible, or at least all the necessary, overarching perspectives from which human behaviour can be understood have been discovered, there is no further need to question our understanding or to push the frontiers of our understanding in search of new ones. (Slife and Williams, 1995: 118)

In general, you are negative, disbelieving, fault-finding, defiant. You do have a big attitude problem. What you probably do not know, what you probably can learn, is how to go from this grumbling negative state along the journey to creative new ideas. You can start with a state of 'I don't agree. I cannot go along with this. What they are saying is nonsense. My reaction is a big "No". I don't like what they are saying.' And you can find ways of using that reaction to search for creative new ideas. You may not know these ways yet, but they are available.

In the meantime, you are wallowing in your big attitude problem, and there is much more to your big attitude problem.

1.2 You do not get caught in the 'language trap': if you use their language, you will think the way they think

Your attitude problem is that you don't let yourself get trapped in the 'language trap', and therefore they say that you have an attitude problem. Since the language trap is so very powerful, and so very insidious, I want to first try to be clear about what the language trap is, how and why it is so dangerous. Then I want to try to be clear about how to spot and to avoid the trap.

What is the language trap? How and why is it so dangerous? Almost every technical term or phrase is loaded with its own implicit conceptual baggage. If you accept and use the technical term or phrase, you are almost automatically accepting the underlying conceptual baggage (Mahrer, 2001b; Whitehead, 1929). There is a quiet war in which each language system wants you to accept its words because then you are thinking in terms of the hidden and implicit way of thinking that goes with the words of that language system (Feyerabend, 1978; Rorty, 1991).

In the time of Pythagoras, the prevailing conceptual system held that the body was composed of four humors: blood, phlegm, yellow bile and black bile, and the fashionable personality category system was based on the idea that personalities were manifestations of the dominant component of the combination or mixture of the four humors. Accordingly, the choleric person was driven by yellow bile. If you described a person as 'choleric,' you were thereby accepting the underlying conceptual system of the four humors of the body.

If, however, you were living in the 1600s or 1700s, you were much too sophisticated to get trapped into diagnosing or officially describing a person as choleric because your conceptual system stamped the four humors of the body as outmoded, quaint, unscientific. Instead, your conceptual personal system was physiologically based, and your sophisticated scientific language enabled you to diagnose or formally describe a person as 'liverish', as having 'the vapors', as being 'nervous'. Of course, if you bought into and used these terms and phrases, you had bought into the underlying conceptual system of the 1600s and 1700s (Richards, 1996).

What about today? If you diagnosed a person, or formally described your patient or your research subject, as choleric or having the vapors, you would probably see some raised eyebrows among the reviewers on the editorial board, the members of your thesis committee, the supervisor of your training program, the reviewers of your proposal for research funding, the other members of the case conference, or the third parties whom you expect to pay you for your professional expertise. Very few of these people would be likely to accept the conceptual baggage that goes along with the term or phrase 'choleric' or 'having the vapors'.

Instead, use terms and phrases such as having seasonal affective disorder, schizophrenia, identity diffusion, fixated at the anal stage, having permeable cognitions, having a depressive disorder. Or try 'anhedonia'. It has been fashionable in the time of Pythagoras, in the 1600s and the 1700s, and today. Use the fashionably professional and scientific terms and phrases, and you have quietly swallowed their underlying conceptual baggage. You are just as vulnerable today. Perhaps more so.

If you use the formal and official diagnostic system of mental illnesses and disorders, you are inadvertently buying into the entire conceptual system that is built into and underlies the formal and official diagnostic system (Follette and Houte, 1996). You are brainwashed.

The trap is so clever. Instead of people being forthright and asking whether you accept the system of mental illnesses and disorders, you are simply to use the system, and when you use the system you have been tricked into accepting the mental illnesses and disorders as well as the hidden conceptual baggage that goes with them.

For example, you are inadvertently accepting 'schizophrenia', without ever being directly asked whether you accept schizophrenia, when you are diverted into using the term, studying schizophrenia, putting schizophrenia to use in answering questions such as the following:

- What are the categories of schizophrenia?
- What is the status of research on schizophrenia?

- What are the new developments in the treatment of schizophrenia?
- What are the symptoms of schizophrenia?
- What are the demographics of schizophrenia with regard to age, sex, nationality, culture?
- What are the causes of schizophrenia?
- How do schizophrenics, normals, and people with other mental disorders compare and contrast in regard to such variables as internal–external control, effectance motivation, problem-solving ability, cognitive permeability, dominance–submissiveness, bilateral transfer, the nature and structure of the amygdala?

You have been tricked if you get to work trying to answer the questions. This version of the trap is clever. It can be used to get you to swallow almost any term or phrase, including devil possession, wandering wombs, elves and goblins, witches and warlocks, stages of development, tears in the working alliance, female empowerment, core cognitive schemata, and schizophrenia.

Almost every technical term and phrase is like an inviting trap. Use it, use the terms and words of a given language system, and you have thereby swallowed its foundational beliefs, its world view, its way of making sense of the relations between a person and the world, its notions of what a person is like, its built-in value system. You have bought its theory, its underlying way of thinking, and you have succumbed painlessly, innocently, without knowing how very much you have swallowed without knowing.

Pick any of the thousands of technical words and phrases of the many language systems that are around and that invite you to use their words and phrases. Use the phrase 'sexual deviant', and you have quietly accepted a whole range of conceptual baggage that goes with that phrase, from valuing ways of being and behaving that are considered 'normal' to notions about 'psychopathology', from the structure of personality to the goals of psychotherapy. Be careful. If you use the phrase 'sexual deviant', you may have little or no idea of just how much extra you have innocently bought. You have been tricked. Be careful.

My friend told about her patient's having been in a prison in a foreign country, and then being released with no explanation. 'And what do you think his conditioned response was? I want your ideas because I found his response was so revealing.' I had trouble answering because I don't think in terms of 'conditioned responses'. If I did, I would also be accepting an organized web of notions and ideas that underlie and go with a conditioned response. In short, the description of a response as "conditioned" has a built-in explanation, namely that it was caused by conditioning factors' (Erwin,

1997: 121). 'Conditioned response' is a loaded phrase. Are you prepared to buy everything that goes with 'conditioned response'?

If your colleague is a card-carrying hermeneuticist, you know you can insidiously poison your colleague's conceptual system by getting your colleague to go along with a deliciously innocent little word: 'subjective'. Without much fanfare, say, 'Most people seem to have their own subjective view on things' or 'He lives mostly in his own subjective world.' If your colleague accepts your statement as having meaning, perhaps even comments in return, you are slowly defeating your colleague's hermeneutic conceptual system. You have inserted an alien concept of a 'subjective world', and that may be like a cancer in your colleague's way of thinking. 'To have a subjective world is to imply that there is an objective world, and the hermeneuticist specifically denies that the world can be divided into these two realms' (Slife and Williams, 1995: 89). Be careful. Technical terms and phrases may be dangerous to the health of your way of thinking.

The language trap can start with what is dressed as a general truth that has face value as being generally true. For example, 'the whole is greater than the sum of its parts.' But be careful. If you buy this general truth, you are also buying virtually all of the direct implications and applications of the general truth that parts gain their function by being part of a larger whole. Koffka (1935), Wertheimer (1944) and Koehler (1947) used this ploy in setting forth the basic tenets of Gestalt theory, so that if you accept the general truth you are virtually accepting Gestalt theory. However, in a careful analysis of the supposed general truth, Madden (1953) concluded that the general truth was not generally true, even as used in Gestalt theory, and he (p. 567) walked away shaking his head about the supposed general truth: 'When Wertheimer claims that the intrinsic nature of the parts is determined by their being in a whole, we must confess that we do not know what he means.' Be careful, you are probably buying a lot more than a general truth, and the truth may well be that the general truth itself is just not true. Be careful of the general truths and of the direct implications and applications of the general truth.

Suppose that you know all of this. You are aware of all this. You are able to see the language trap before it springs, before you are trapped. What can you do to avoid getting caught in the language trap? Just seeing it reaching for you is not enough. You must do something more.

When you see the language trap, perhaps the best way to avoid getting trapped is to decline, stay away, shine a light on the trap. For example, if you are talking over a case, and the presenter says, 'She is showing symptoms of schizophrenia, right?', you may politely avoid getting trapped by saying that you have no idea because 'schizophrenia' makes no sense in your way of thinking. You may pleasantly declare yourself out of the group because schizophrenia is something you know nothing about. You may show your confusion about the meaning of schizophrena in relation to words and phrases such as being a lunatic, lost her mind, being crazy, off her rocker, being deranged. You may make a spectacle of yourself by protesting, in your own words, 'Wait a minute! You want me to accept the whole idea of schizophrenia? You want me to think in your approach, your way of thinking? No! No! If I think in your system, I have to give up my way of thinking! No way! You are brainwashing me!' You may even vainly try to explain what you understand as the language trap you are trying to avoid getting trapped in. Or you may use some other way of not getting caught in the language trap.

However, there are risks, penalties to be paid, if you dare to avoid getting caught in the language trap. One penalty is that you are letting yourself in for more pressure: 'Come on, you know what we mean.' 'Everyone knows what "schizophrenia" is.' Another penalty is that you are asking for criticism: 'You are resistant.' 'You are weird.' 'You are so hard to talk to.' 'You are so rebellious.' 'You are so sensitive about words.' 'No one can talk to you.' A third penalty is that you are not allowed to get what you want to get unless you play their language game. Your manuscript will be rejected. Your request for funding will be denied. You will not be accepted into the program. You will not get the job. You will not be promoted.

In other words, if you use their words, their terms and phrases, you are swallowing their way of thinking. If you know about and spot the language trap, and avoid getting caught, you have a big attitude problem. Hooray for the big attitude problem!

1.3 *You have a childlike fascination with the creation of new ideas*
You have spent your life in the world of creative new ideas. This is your world. It was your world when you were a child. It has always been your world. You may have been a dreamer or a doer or both, but you have always lived in this world of unending wonder and surprise, of excitement and fascination. It is your personal world.

Coming up with creative new ideas is so central to your being, so much a part of who and what you are, that it can become a whole new matter to step aside from being you and to try to think of yourself as creative, as being a wellspring of creative new ideas. It is as if you stop being the creative you when you try to put yourself in a position of thinking of yourself as a creative person. Yet there can be some qualities that go along with being a creative person.

It can seem that you possess a quality of self-confidence, of almost unwavering faith and trust, of arrogant superiority in your ability to come up with creative new ideas. Whatever the challenge, whether it is big or little, grandiose or practical and mundane, you have a boundless certainty of your ability to come up with creative new ideas. Being this way is merely being you.

Because of your childlike fascination with creative new ideas, it is almost natural for you to think of the field of psychotherapy theory, research, practice and training as gloriously evolving, advancing, improving, changing. It is your nature to think in terms of exciting new developments, of unexplored new territories, of cascading unfoldings, of never-ending future possibilities.

1.4 You can be utterly wrong

You are able to acknowledge that your creative new ideas are wrong, that what you believe is wrong, flawed, inadequate, inferior. Being wrong is, for you, accompanied by feelings that are pleasant, exciting, rather than grudging, defensive, bad.

You can welcome evidence that you are wrong. You are able to accept the challenge of seeing whether what you believe is true or useful, is untrue and essentially useless, wrong, is to be let go of, discarded, abandoned. You can put on the table the reasonable evidence that you would accept as sufficient for you to give up what you believe, and you can take the next honorable step of letting go of what you believe if the evidence is indeed sufficient (Mahrer, 2003). For example,

> If it were to turn out that the physical mechanisms that completely explain human behaviour at no level exhibited the structure of beliefs and desires, then something we had all along believed, viz., that beliefs and desires were among the causes of behaviour, would turn out to be false. (Loar, 1981: 14)

You are ready and willing to give up notions and ideas that you believe. There can be sufficient evidence for you to do so.

You can be wrong without the world falling apart, without the awful turmoil of crashing pillars. If you have believed that the world is truly flat, you can be wrong. If you know that the world is round, you can be wrong. And the state of being wrong is pleasant. Something new can happen. What is next? For most people, being wrong is dreadful, unthinkable. The very possibility of giving up a cherished truth means plunging into an abyss of utter chaos, awful ambiguity, free-falling terror, nothing to cling to. But not for you, not for the creative person.

One part of your attitude problem is that you can be utterly wrong, you can give up what you have believed, and you can do so without falling apart, without getting twisted into some awful shape. Those who are more ordinary, more normal, will probably be bothered by your graceful willingness to be utterly wrong. They may see you as frivolous, as not truly believing, as not being devoted to what you believe, as not being trustworthy, as not really believing in anything. In a sense, they are right.

1.5 You love wallowing in the utterly unknown

You are drawn, like a magnet, to the utterly unknown, to the world of the inexplicable, the unpredictable, the unexpected. You can be found, wandering around like a fascinated child, in a part of the world that is essentially unknown. When you come to a fork in the road, with one option known and the other leading toward the unknown, you are captivated by following the unknown option.

You love wallowing around in the utterly unknown, simply because the unknown is fascinating. The fascination of the utterly unknown is far more important than seeking to shock others, to rebel, to resist doing the normal and the ordinary, to go where you are told not to go, to defy restrictions, to violate rules and regulations, to go against warnings, prohibitions, interdictions. You wallow in the utterly unknown simply because it is absolutely fascinating wallowing in the utterly unknown.

Almost everyone desperately clings to being the essential person that one is, allowing distal and superficial changes in anything that is outside the essential self, the core of one's I-ness, but keeping sacrosanct and out of bounds anything that can actually touch one's precious I-ness. In stark contrast, you are entranced with hurling yourself into complete and utter transformation, into sacrificing every shred of the very person you are and becoming whatever qualitatively new person you can become. You are ready to sacrifice the 'you' who you are and to become an entirely new 'you'. Here is another world in which you can love wallowing in the utterly unknown.

There is an outer periphery of what is known, an outer boundary. Some theoreticians and researchers are working at the outer boundary, pushing it out a bit, extending it here and there, moving it further out. They are generally careful, inventive, creative, gathering more knowledge for the cumulative body of knowledge. For you, that outer boundary is like a springboard that can launch you far into the depths of the whole fantasy world of the utterly unknown. Instead of its being the outer boundary of what is known, that line is the entrance into your wonderful world of the utterly unknown.

If there is a creative new idea floating by, you are drawn toward it, you can play with it, you can give it a friendly reception, you are welcoming toward it. A creative new idea is fun for you, is enjoyable. You can play with it. You may not actually buy the creative new idea, but you can at least consider it. Your knee-jerk reaction is not one of closing up, having to be persuaded by mounds of convincing proof. For example, you can allow yourself to be face to face with a creative new idea called 'volition', and you can consider it rather than forcing it to parade a powerful research case on its behalf:

> If we assume that the discipline is strongly Skinnerian (1987), operating from the assumption that mentalistic concepts are unnecessary in the science of psychology, then one needs strong and pervasive evidence indeed for volition. But large segments of psychology, especially following the hegemony of the cognitive revolution, do not require such strong evidence for human agency and volition. The Bayesian consensus (i.e., the paradigm) is already inclined toward that conclusion. (Borgen, 1992: 125)

1.6 You can 'leave the unfamiliar be', rather than converting it into an alien threat or reducing it to the familiar

To begin with, you have an ability to see the unfamiliar in the first place. You can see something as out of the ordinary, exceptional, unusual, unfamiliar. That alone is a somewhat rare quality (Schon, 1982). I am not picturing the general outlook of a naive child for whom almost anything and everything can be fresh, new, captivating, unusual. Instead, I am merely picturing that you can see something as relatively unfamiliar. Just seeing it is enough.

You are further able to 'leave the unfamiliar be', to keep it there before you. You can attend to it, observe it, look at it. You are able to leave it be as something interesting, different, beyond the familiar, perhaps as something curious, puzzling, inexplicable. You are able to give it your attention, perhaps to merely appreciate it, perhaps to touch it, tinker a bit with it, maybe play with it. But you are able to leave the unfamiliar be.

You can start by accepting it as unfamiliar. What this paragraph is saying is truly unfamiliar. That shimmering cube, hovering in the air, is truly unfamiliar. And you are able to wait, to give it some time. See what presents itself. Be ready to receive whatever comes, whenever it becomes. Be moderately expectant that something will come, but you will probably not know what it will be. You are just here, waiting, giving presence to the unfamiliar.

You are the kind of person who does not almost automatically convert it into an alien threat, something bad, threatening, dangerous, ominous, something to be drawn back from, distanced, protected from. You do not instantly label it as crazy, bizarre, lunatic, out of its mind, bedeviled, as demonic diablerie. You do not spring into action to treat it, do something about it, make it normal, surround it with prohibitions and interdictions. You do not automatically marginalize it, trivialize it, sideline it, overlook it, dismiss it. You are not galvanized into attacking it, twisting it out of shape, imprisoning it, killing it.

You are the kind of person who can leave the unfamiliar be, rather than automatically reducing it to what is familiar. You don't have to classify it with familiar classifications, describe it with familiar descriptions, categorize it with familiar categorizations, identify it with familiar identifications. Doing this is common, automatic and instantaneous, but it is not leaving the unfamiliar be.

I played the first 15 minutes and the last 15 minutes of a tape of a 90-minute session. The six psychotherapists were so impressed with the magical change that they genuinely wondered whether this was a trick, whether the tape had been spliced, whether the patient was really an actor participating in a practical joke. When the six psychotherapists were reassured that the tape was genuine, untampered with, they were both excited and skeptical about what had brought about such an impressive change in the session.

I then played the middle section of the tape. When they had heard the unusual things that the therapist and client had done to help bring about the amazing changes, five of the six psychotherapists sputtered, interrupted one another in pasting familiar labels on what was so very unfamiliar. They belted out phrases like 'emotional flooding', 'That was paradoxical intention', 'hypnotic techniques', 'EMDR!', 'symptom intensification', 'Existentialists wrote about that', 'multiple personality'. It was as if five of the six psychotherapists had said, 'We are totally unfamiliar with what we just heard, so we will "reduce it to the familiar" by using familiar labels, categories and phrases. Then we can avoid being bowled over by what we really don't understand.'

The sixth psychotherapist did not participate in the defensive yelling of labels. When the other five psychotherapists had quieted down, reassuring themselves that their labels made the unfamiliar familiar, she said, 'Can I borrow that tape? I would like to study it. Something very special happened there. I am impressed.'

Her colleagues made fun of her for being so impressed. They wondered whether she disagreed with their labels, descriptions. They were critical of her interest in the tape.

Her colleagues had to convert what they had heard into an alien threat. Her colleagues had successfully reduced the unfamiliar to familiar labels and categories. Her colleagues were probably not ready to have creative new ideas. In contrast, she was able to leave the unfamiliar be. She could appreciate that there was probably something special here, and she was drawn toward taking a closer look. Her unwillingness to join her colleagues in seeing whatever happened as an alien threat, her unwillingness to reduce whatever happened to familiar labels and categories, and her eagerness to study the tape, all showed that this psychotherapist had a big attitude problem. Her colleagues were right.

These contrasting mind-sets have been examined by philosophers of science. One mind-set is open to and appreciative of the unfamiliar, the new, the strange. The other mind-set is more inclined to see the unfamiliar as an alien threat,' something to be quickly reduced to the familiar. Duhem (1996) discussed these two mind-sets in giving his impressions of many French and German physicists, on the one hand, as contrasted with many English physicists, on the other hand. French and German physicists were inclined to be suspicious and critical of what might be unfamiliar, strange, new, out of the ordinary. In contrast, English physicists seemed drawn toward, to enjoy and appreciate what seemed new and unfamiliar, extraordinary:

> French and German physicists ... will not tolerate either contradictions or gaps in their theories. Consequently, it seems to them that any proposition not clearly and evidently connected with accepted principles, any that is strange, any that is surprising, must be called into question for that very reason. Matters are completely different with the English. Strange things do not frighten them. Surprises do not create doubt for them. They seem, on the contrary, to seek out all that is unforseen and all that is audacious in the domain of science. (ibid: 69)

There are those, like my five colleagues, who have trouble leaving the unfamiliar be, and who must see the unfamiliar as an alien threat to be reduced to the familiar by means of familiar labels and categories. They are unlikely to come up with creative new ideas. There are those, like my sixth colleague who borrowed the tape, who are able to leave the unfamiliar be, who can be drawn toward and can appreciate the unfamiliar. She is ready to have creative new ideas. I am so thankful for those rare colleagues who have this precious kind of big attitude problem.

1.7 You love arousing, challenging, violating the crowd – more in a spirit of revolution than rebellion

It is almost a rule that creative new ideas will be opposed by the main body of the field. Old established traditions are old, established and traditional. They are generally supported by the authorities, by the important theorists and researchers, and taken for granted by the crowd. Creative new ideas face a generally hostile audience 'in that all available evidence speaks overwhelmingly against them' (Feigl, 1953: 12).

For most people, this state of affairs can be rather menacing and scary. It dampens attempts to come up with truly creative ideas. The reception will be hostile. However, for the truly creative person, this state of affairs is grist to the mill because the truly creative person loves arousing, challenging, violating the crowd, loves uprooting what the crowd takes for granted, as basically true.

In arousing the crowd, the spirit is one of revolution, of a whole new way of thinking and doing, of uprooting the old and making room for the new, of challenging this direction in favor of that direction. This is the underlying spirit, rather than a nasty spirit of merely opposing, fighting against, protesting against, criticizing and attacking mainly to criticize and attack, a spirit of negative rebelliousness. It is a spirit of exciting revolution, rather than of mean-spirited rebelliousness.

Coming up with creative new ideas is helped if you have a readiness for coming up with creative new ideas, and this readiness is helped if you are a person with a big attitude problem. But having a big attitude problem is probably not sufficient all by itself. There is something more to be truly ready.

2. Here is a test of readiness to have creative new ideas

There are eight chapters in this volume. Each chapter includes three to five or so methods of coming up with creative ideas. As you read about each method, please try to read in a spirit filled with questions such as these: do I understand this method? does it make some sense to me? does it appeal to me? have I done anything like this method? do I want to carry out this method? Please try to give each method a fair hearing, a chance to speak to you, to present its case.

You have passed the test if, before you finished reading about all the methods, or after you finished reading about them all, you actually engaged in learning and using at least one of the methods. You spent at least a few hours actively carrying out some method, and you did this within a month or so of reading about the method. You passed the test of readiness to have creative new ideas.

You fail the test if your knee-jerk reaction, your almost instant reaction to what you are reading, goes well beyond reasonable consideration and sensible challenging, beyond a fair weighing of what is presented. There can be no reasonable evidence that could convince you of the worth of the methods. The methods must be attacked. The examples cannot be allowed to stand. You must find fault, see fatal flaws, dismiss what you are reading. You fail the test, not because you are unconvinced by what you read, but rather because there can be no reasonable way for you to allow a fair hearing. This is one way to fail the test.

You fail the test if, after starting to read about the methods, a few months or a few years go by and you haven't engaged in learning and using any of the methods. This is the test.

3. You should be reasonably competent in the special skills of creating new ideas

You may well believe that being 'creative' is just about enough for you to be able to come up with creative new ideas, especially if you are also smart. I am more inclined to believe that being blessed with this inner spark of creativity is necessary but it is not enough. I also believe you have to have the right kinds of actual skills. The rest of this volume spells out these right kinds of actual skills.

Each of the methods is described in sufficient detail for you to be able to carry it out. The description of each of the methods includes examples. The descriptions and the examples can give you a reasonably clear picture of what the method is. Learning them is up to you.

Learning these skills also takes work. It calls for learning, for practice. Merely skimming through the various skills is probably not enough for the person to be good enough, to be sufficiently competent, to come up with creative new ideas. It seems to take repetitive, down-to-earth practice, training, skill-learning to be sufficiently competent to come up with creative new ideas.

3.1 A training program is good if it includes study and learning of the special skills of coming up with creative new ideas

Picture a course that is explicitly designed to show students how to develop creative new ideas in the field of psychotherapy theory, research, practice and training, a course aimed at developing the actual skills to be introduced and described in the remainder of this work.

If a training program includes the development of these skills, the training program is good. My impression is that there are precious few training programs that can provide solid evidence that they include this component. That is too bad.

If you are a teacher in the field of psychotherapy, if you are an administrator or a student, if you are in any position to change training programs even a little bit, I hope that you can do something to include this component in at least some training programs. In this sense, you can do something to help advance the training of future psychotherapists and the field as a whole.

If you are interested in a particular one of the following skills, actually try it out. Spend an hour or so actually trying it out. Keep going until you can become reasonably proficient in the particular skill. Then move on to the next explicit skill that interests you.

If you are a teacher, take some time to figure out useful training exercises for each of the skills that interests you. Then give students an opportunity to go through each of the exercises so as to improve their level of proficiency in each of the skills.

It takes more than just 'getting the idea' for each of the following explicit skills. It takes training. It takes skill-learning to become reasonably proficient in being able to come up with creative new ideas.

CHAPTER 2

Go Outside or Inside the Crowd

I am inclined to picture most psychotherapists as part of the mainstream. They have the more or less accepted degrees, belong to the relatively common organizations and associations, have the generally accepted licenses and registrations, adhere to the profession's standards and codes, are proponents of the more common schools or approaches to psychotherapy. They are the relatively mainstream practitioners, theorists, researchers, teachers and trainers, and administrators. They have all sorts of differences from one another, by no means think and act in a single fashion, and yet they represent the mainstream of the science and profession of psychotherapy.

When I refer to these people as the 'crowd', it is with a mixture of mildly positive and mildly negative feelings. I picture the crowd of psychotherapists as something pleasant to be part of, to belong to. They help define my identity. They help give me a sense of history, a part of my professional identity. Relative to other 'crowds', my crowd keeps me somewhat safe, helps preserve me and what I do. I like my crowd. I could easily use the phrase 'professional group' when I have these positive feelings.

On the other hand, there are ways in which I do think of my professional group as a crowd. Merely by being a professional group, it sets and enforces standards, defines what psychotherapists are generally to believe and to know, has the power to accredit or not accredit my training program, to give me or not give me a license to practice, to represent the way most psychotherapists are to think, to act, to work. I can think of my professional group as a crowd

31

with some power and clout. It might be able to swallow me up. It might be able to hurt me. I don't think it will, but it is possible.

I can be part of the 'crowd' that makes up the mainstream of psychotherapists, and the accompanying feeling can be good and positive or somewhat uneasy and negative.

Some psychotherapists are outside the mainstream, outside the crowd. They may or may not be outside the crowd on a fulltime basis, and they may show that they are indeed a part of the crowd in some ways and outside the crowd in some other ways. They need not be rebellious nonconformists, fighting the establishment, but they might be. Typically, these are psychotherapists who do not usually attend the mainstream conventions, spend much time with mainstream psychotherapists, read mainstream journals and books, work in mainstream departments or agencies. They may pride themselves on being outside the mainstream, outside the crowd, or they may not. Yet there seem to be some psychotherapists who, in one way or another, to some degree or another, are outside the mainstream, outside the crowd of most psychotherapists.

This chapter deals with psychotherapists who are generally either inside or outside the mainstream, the professional group, the crowd, and I acknowledge that the word 'crowd' can have a mildly negative value pinned to it.

I also acknowledge that, when it comes to creative new ideas, what I refer to as the mainstream, the professional group, the crowd can be downright menacing. It can make big trouble for psychotherapists who bear the gift of creative new ideas. It can stifle creative new ideas. It can wield powerful forces to discourage, prevent, punish the venture for creative new ideas. It can force psychotherapists to think the way the crowd demands that psychotherapists think. The crowd can be scary, both for psychotherapists inside the crowd and for psychotherapists who are outside. When I picture the crowd this way, I acknowledge that I think of the crowd as more of a 'mob'. But this is an extreme word and brings pictures that may well be unfair. On the other hand, when I picture the crowd of mainstream psychotherapists exerting powerful pressure to think and act like the crowd, I am inclined to think of the crowd as more of a herd of psychotherapists moving along as a single large force, group.

I will be referring to the mainstream of psychotherapists as the crowd, rather than the professional group, the science and profession of psychotherapy. Occasionally, when I picture the crowd as menacing and ominous, I will use the word 'herd'.

In any case, coming up with creative new ideas can be helped by two back-to-back guidelines: (a) If you are essentially inside the crowd, go outside the crowd, exit, leave, take a vacation from being inside the crowd, see what it can be like wholly outside the crowd. (b) If you are essentially outside the crowd, join the crowd, become a part of the crowd, mingle, enjoy, work and play with the crowd, talk and be with the crowd, challenge and be challenged by the crowd.

1. If you are inside the crowd, go outside

When you are inside the crowd, you almost certainly think the way the crowd thinks. You are a part of the crowd. You think the way you think without usually being able to say that you think the way you think because you are part of the crowd. In a sense, you share the group mentality, but without knowing that you share the group mentality. It is as if you are part of a crowd that hypnotizes you into not knowing that you are part of the crowd.

The road to creative new ideas starts with your getting outside the crowd, freeing yourself of the unwitting sense of sharing what the crowd thinks. It is like struggling to know that you are living and being in a dream world. It is like waking up from a state in which you are sharing the crowd mentality. Wanting to go outside the crowd is an expression of the beginning of being free of the crowd. Actually being free of the crowd can put you outside the stultifying effects of being part of the crowd, of having the crowd mentality, and put you in a place where you can be more open to creative new ideas.

There can be several ways to go outside the crowd:

1.1 Hurl yourself into a wholesale fantasy of a whole new world
One way of getting outside the crowd is to actively enter into the proper state. Living and being in the crowd, you are living and being in one state. The way out is to exit this ordinary state and enter into a qualitatively different right state. It is the difference between a sleeping state and a waking state. It is a qualitative shift.

Exiting out of the state of being inside the crowd calls for two steps (Mahrer, 2000a). The first step is reciting, over and over again, and convincing yourself, with pounding loudness and enthusiasm: 'There is a whole different way of thinking, a whole new way of thinking about and seeing things! Everything I have presumed is wrong! It is limited and wrong! There is a whole new outlook, a whole different way of seeing things and making sense of things!' Keep saying this over and over, with increasing loudness and volume, with more and more energy.

The second step is to hurl yourself into thoroughly wild speculation, wholesale fantasy, unrestrained conjecture and all about all things psychological. Let go of all reality constraints. Without pausing, throw yourself into utter flights of fantasy. Raise the stakes as high as possible by engaging in utter nonsense. Plunge into wild new worlds of the impossible. Go wilder and wilder. Enter the world of the utterly fictitious, the crazy and unrestrained, the wild and the lunatic and all in regard to everything psychological, to the world of psychological things, to how and why people are the way they are, to what people are like, to how people can change, to what people can become, to every issue and secret in and beyond the field of psychotherapy.

By following these two steps, you are putting yourself into a state of being out of the crowd. The first step is dismissing everything that is taken for granted as true as not really true at all and welcoming a whole new way of thinking. The second step is throwing yourself into a whole new world of wholesale fantasy, especially in regard to issues of the field of psychotherapy. When these two steps are done fully and well, you are out of the herd mentality, you have succeeded in going outside the way most people think.

1.2 Visit, study and learn from neighboring fields

Many of the grand new ideas in the field of psychotherapy originated in neighboring fields and then worked their way into the field of psychotherapy. I am referring to most of the grand new ideas in the field, from dream analysis to statistical analysis, from stages of development to psychopathology, from unconscious agencies to the helping alliance, from logical positivism to behaviorism, from postmodernism to constructivism, from empiricism to phenomenology, from cognitivism to hermeneutics.

You can get out of the crowd, the herd mentality, by visiting, studying and learning from neighboring fields. Go to these neighboring fields in search of the fashionable current new ideas there. Learn the grand new ideas percolating in these other fields. Become a student of what is truly new in these neighboring fields.

You may read little or nothing about what is current in the field of psychotherapy. Or you may attend some conferences, glance through a journal occasionally, read a chapter here and there. In any case, the invitation is to take an active step toward seeing what is current in a neighboring field. Ask someone who knows about postmodernism or robotics or marine biology or the theory of relativity what you can do to have a simple introduction to what is currently fashionable in that field. You are an uneducated outsider looking for a resource aimed at telling uneducated outsiders some of the fashionable new ideas in the field, and aimed at doing so simply, nontechnically, for the interested non-sophisticate, the unknowledgeable outsider.

Visit, study and learn from neighboring fields, from cultural anthropology to philosophy, from artificial intelligence to epistemology, from religion to ontology, from physics to hermeneutics, from astronomy to linguistics and semantics, from mathematics to logic and reasoning. When you truly wallow in the new ideas in these neighboring fields, you have succeeded in extricating yourself from the crowd of psychotherapists, from the common mainstream in psychotherapy.

1.3 Study philosophy of science to see how it can bear creative implications for the field of psychotherapy

Of all the neighboring fields, philosophy of science is probably the one that can most easily lift you outside the field of psychotherapy. Start with a text from philosophy of science, and consider following two steps to get you outside the field of psychotherapy.

The first step is to read with a readiness to see how this particular point might apply to some issue or point, some concrete matter, in the field of psychotherapy. As you read a sentence or a paragraph, keep in mind pictures from the field of psychotherapy. Picture psychotherapy researchers figuring out what to do their research on, coming up with an hypothesis, selecting some design or methodology. Picture a person having a feeling that is bothersome. Picture a therapist having a stream of private inferences. Picture a therapist trying to put into words what the client is saying or meaning. Keep these pictures in your mind, off to the side, as you read the sentence or paragraph. In other words, as you read a paragraph of philosophy of science, try to keep in mind pictures of what ordinarily takes place in the field of psychotherapy practice and research, theorizing and teaching.

The second step is to grasp the point of the sentence or paragraph, and then ask yourself how this point can affect the field of psychotherapy, how this point could make a difference in the field of psychotherapy, what the implications might be for the field of psychotherapy. Ask yourself, 'What might be the creative, new, interesting, important implications of this point, this notion or idea, for the field of psychotherapy?'

For example, you are reading philosophy of science, and the text describes how two theories seemed to have done fairly well in solving a problem in mechanics, and both shared a similar concept, though differing in other respects. The text poses the issue of whether a third theory might also solve that problem by adopting the common concept, and the text concludes that the answer is no, because if the third theory adopted the common concept it would have to adopt the underlying and auxiliary conceptual baggage, and that would essentially destroy the third theory by replacing it with a combination of the first two theories. Isn't that interesting?

Now go one step further and ask what implications this point might have for the field of psychotherapy. Even as you begin to see how this philosophy of science point could well have some perhaps sweeping implications for the 'common elements' type of psychotherapy research, you have also managed to extricate yourself from the field of psychotherapy and to place yourself in the shoes of a neighboring field, namely philosophy of science.

Here is a test: you read in philosophy of science about the relativity of motion and of time in the fields of geometry and physics.

> For the geometer, as for the physicist, if a material point were alone in the world, it would be absurd to speak of its motion; what reference would allow this motion to be recognized? We cannot speak of the motion of a material point except by conceiving at the same time the existence of a point of comparison from which it is observed. (Duhem, 1996: 124; cf. Reichenbach, 1953).

And this about time: 'Neither the geometer nor the physicist would be able to talk about an absolute time but only of a time relative to a certain clock' (Duhem, 1996: 125).

Suppose that the point is this: something we take for granted as existent and true is existent and true only relative to something else as a point of comparison. Now do your best to apply this point to the field of psychotherapy theory, research or practice to try to see how this point might have some significant implications. As you are engaged in this attempt, whatever you may come up with, you have succeeded in extricating yourself from the field of psychotherapy.

1.4 Seek out and engage in creative discussions with creative thinkers in other fields

Actively seek out creative thinkers in other fields. You may choose creative thinkers in such neighboring fields as education, philosophy, sociology, theology, artificial intelligence. Or you may choose creative thinkers in fields that are further away, fields such as astrology, mathematics, engineering, physics, chemistry, robotics.

Picture serious discussions with one or two of these creative thinkers, or perhaps a larger group. Discuss their ideas. Discuss your own ideas. By engaging in these kinds of serious discussions with creative thinkers in other fields, you can succeed in lifting yourself outside the field of psychotherapy.

These are four ways that can be successful in taking you outside the ordinary field of psychotherapy. Why is this important? The answer is that if you are inside the herd, the common field of psychotherapy, coming up with creative new ideas can be helped by going outside, and the invitation is to use these and other ways to get outside.

2. If you are outside the crowd, go inside

Many psychotherapists are essentially loners who have little or no direct contact with the established crowd of psychotherapists. They work by themselves in their solo practices or they have jobs where they are the only psychotherapist in the unit or on the floor. When they have ideas about their craft, the ideas come and go, and that is that.

Many psychotherapists have all sorts of ideas that they record as running notes or fragmentary writings that they keep to themselves. Sometimes they write papers, but the papers are not published.

Many psychotherapists cluster with their own non-establishment groups. They are Jungians or Adlerians or logotherapists. They do primal therapy or psychodrama or poetry therapy or psychosynthesis or Morita therapy or psycho-imagination therapy, and they talk to others who belong to the same group. They are not inclined to have much contact with members of other groups, especially with the established crowd, the mainstream, whatever that happens to be.

If psychotherapists do research, it is often on topics that are outside the popular mainstream topics. They do research on lucid dreaming or mystical experiences or automatic writing, and rarely publish in the mainstream journals, if they publish at all.

There are plenty of non-mainstream, special-interest journals and newsletters and publication outlets, but if a Jungian or a logotherapist submits a piece containing truly creative new ideas to a Jungian or a logotherapy outlet, they still must follow house rules for what is allowed or disallowed as creative ideas and for how the ideas are to be acceptably dressed and presented (Chubin and Hackett, 1990; Fuller, 1994, 1996; Paulus, 1989). Often these in-house publication outlets can be tougher than mainstream establishment journals on the unwritten rules for accepting genuinely creative new ideas.

The net result is that it is easy to remain outside the herd, and that may be a common, prudent and safe way to live, but not for the care and feeding of creative new ideas. If you want to have creative new ideas, and if you live and work mainly outside the herd, go inside the herd. There are some interesting ways that going inside the herd can help you to come up with creative new ideas.

2.1 The crowd can push you either to conform or to do some creative new thinking

Outside the crowd, you may or may not be a creative thinker. But when you go inside the crowd, it is likely that you can become a creative thinker.

Meet the crowd. Go to their meetings, their conferences. Attend their workshops. Take their courses, their seminars, their training programs. Participate, join in, be one of them. Spend some time working in their agencies, workplaces, departments. Sit in on their committee meetings. Have coffee with them. Talk with them. Join their chat groups. Be friends with them. Have conversations with them about psychotherapy research, practice, theory, training.

The crowd does not necessarily have a single, uniform way of thinking and doing. There is a range of more or less common and accepted ways of thinking and doing. Of course there is some variability. Not everyone in the establishment is a cognitive behaviorist. Yet the herd is the herd, and there are common and accepted ways of thinking.

When you mingle with the crowd, when you go inside the crowd, the chances are you can face a choice of either adopting its ways or starting to engage in some creative thinking. You are face to face with what the crowd thinks and does, and you are in a special position to crystallize your own way, and perhaps do some creative thinking of your own. Here are the establishment ways of relating to clients, of conducting assessments and evaluations, of doing psychotherapy, of doing research, of doing research on these topics, of making sense of clients and how they got to be the way they are. Do you agree? What are your own ways of dealing with these matters?

By going inside the crowd, you may well find yourself virtually forced to do some creative thinking. The waiting alternative is to fit in, to adopt some mainstream way of thinking about and doing the mainstream things.

2.2 Find a creative new idea by starting from whatever makes the crowd twitch and snarl

If you are outside the crowd, you can come up with creative new ideas by playing a game with three steps. You can start without having a creative new idea. Just follow the three steps and you will come up with some creative new ideas.

Step 1 is to study the crowd at work, carrying on its deliberations, dealing with matters that are theoretical or professional. Study the range of publications on some issue such as how to supervise trainees, how to work with patients who are diagnosed as crazy, new developments in the ways therapists and clients relate and interact with one another, the role of gender in psychotherapy. Sit in on conferences, seminars, committee meetings, interactions between the important people and members of the audience.

Step 2 tells you what to look for. Look for whatever makes the crowd twitch or snarl. There will be times when the crowd will get twitchy, edgy, on guard, vigilant, nervous. The herd is being threatened, bothered, sensing something ominous, menacing. Even more telltale clues are when the herd snarls. Something has violated the herd, provoked the herd's closed mind. The herd snarls, 'You are not permitted to think the way you think. You must think the way we think.'

Pay special attention to times when much of the herd is truly upset, when members of many approaches snarl, when most of the herd is up in arms. 'Someone dares to say that the earth is not the center of the universe? Excommunicate him. Behead him. Stop him from his blasphemy.' When most of the field raise their clenched fists, when most of the field close ranks to do serious harm to the offender, when something strikes a sensitive collective nerve and the collective reacts with extreme anger, you may well be in the vicinity of a creative new idea.

The third step is to figure out what it is that makes the herd so twitchy and snarly. Look for the dangerous idea, the villain, whatever is threatening the herd. Something is making the herd nervous. The herd is defending itself against something, is avoiding and skirting around something, is attacking something. Sometimes it is conspicuous. Sometimes you have to follow the clues to see what it is. Once you can identify what it is, see the creative new idea that is nearby, that is hinted at. See how the threat can point to a creative new idea. This is the third step.

Here are some examples of how it can work. The panel or committee or group is discussing the aims and goals of psychotherapy, its outcomes. After a comment from one member or from the audience, the air is nervous and twitchy, and the panel defends the idea that we, the professional psychotherapists, are the ones whose mandate it is to deal with these aims and goals. Something is amiss. Something is in the air. The implied enemy idea is that meditation is a scholarly and traditional owner of many of the loftier aims and goals. The herd is arguing against this without arguing openly against this idea.

Start from here and see if you can discover a creative new idea lurking in the shadows. Think. Then you find a possibility. Perhaps the aims and goals of the field of psychotherapy are quite limited and restricted; perhaps there are aims and goals that are loftier, more elevated, on a higher plateau than those of the field of psychotherapy; perhaps the field of psychotherapy would be advanced considerably if it adopted these loftier aims and goals.

The group was reporting about charges against a fellow who pretended to be a professional psychotherapist and had maintained a practice for nine years. Then the atmosphere became nervous and tense, twitchy and snarly, when it was indicated that he had not finished high school, had worked in refrigeration for a decade, opened his practice of psychotherapy, was written up in the newspaper of a large city for his achievements with many patients who were severely depressed. How dare he masquerade as a professional psychotherapist!

Searching from here for the creative new idea led to this possibility: could it be that the many years of professional training of psychotherapy were essentially worthless? Could it be that some people can 'do psychotherapy' just as well or better than most professional psychotherapists, even without this training? Who are the real offenders, those who just do psychotherapy with no training at all or those who masquerade as 'professional psychotherapists'?

There is a roundtable discussion of the advances in psychotherapy over the past three or four decades, and everything is peaceful and calm until something happens and the discussion becomes nervous and ominous. The atmosphere switches, and it is as if the discussion is insisting that the field of psychotherapy is empirically based, is grounded in research, is indeed a science. There is an unseen enemy, lurking about in the air. It is as if the group is responding to an unvoiced accusation that the field is not empirically based, has convinced itself that it is grounded in research, is not really a science at all. Following these clues, the creative new idea is that somehow, in some way, perhaps the field of psychotherapy has a long way to go to qualify as a legitimate science; perhaps the field is a pseudo-science that hides itself behind scientific-sounding terms and methods. Perhaps the field can truly advance when it can take giant steps toward adopting the ways and means of what scientific fields accept as genuine science.

When the panel or committee or group, when the establishment in-group, when the important people can tolerate and welcome lots of different ideas, exceptions, possibilities, you tend to lose the opportunity to see what can make them wince, recoil, close ranks, twitch and snarl. It is a sense of 'Let's be open to whatever appears and be willing to talk about just about anything that is on the table to talk about.' The state of openness tends to defeat the possibility of catching whatever threatens the crowd.

On the other hand, if you can see the crowd become tight, get nervous, growl, send up danger signals, twitch and snarl, you may be on to something.

You may be able to track down the dangerous threat, and that dangerous threat just may be a creative new idea.

2.3 Develop and hone creative new ideas through one-on-one encounters with the crowd

If you are outside the crowd, playing with some creative new idea, enter into the crowd and put the creative new idea to the test. If you have practiced the cello by yourself, see how you do with the great cellists of symphonies. If you learned how to box in local gyms, see how well you do when you fight against the highly ranked professionals. If you have painted by yourself, see how your paintings do in big-time galleries. If you have written notes, put them in the form of actual publications and submit them to the crowd's journals.

Go ahead and engage in one-on-one encounters with the crowd. Actually debate against the establishment. Take on the important people in the establishment. Test out your creative new ideas against the crowd.

By means of one-on-one encounters with the crowd, your ideas can develop, can clarify, can grow, can modify. You can hone your creative ideas. They take better shape. They can be sharpened, refined, improved.

When you engage in one-on-one encounters with the crowd, you can meet others who rebel, who have alternative ideas, who take on the crowd. You can become a part of some other movement or you can see that your creative new ideas stand apart from the others, are distinctive from the other creative new ideas.

New ideas tend to develop and grow when you engage in one-on-one encounters with the crowd, in meetings and conversations with the crowd, in sparring matches with the crowd, in the stimulation of give and take with the establishment. This gives your ideas better form and shape. This challenges your ideas to rise to the occasion. This invites further and better ideas. In general, the crowd can be a wonderful crucible for developing and honing your own ideas into better and more creative new ideas.

2.4 Ideas that are common and accepted outside the crowd can be excitingly novel and creative inside the crowd

In your own little group, outside the crowd, there are some ideas that are relatively common and accepted. They are ordinary and normal. However, something dramatic can happen when you go inside the crowd. First of all, those common and accepted ideas are not at all common and accepted in the crowd. Instead, those ideas are new, different, distinctive. Secondly, by being new and different, they can give rise to more and more new ideas in the context of the crowd.

You are part of a group that does meditation. Almost everyone in your group does meditation for about 30 minutes a day, every day, and most of you have done meditation for about 10 years or more. Meditation is common and accepted in your group.

Suppose that you and your group go to a psychotherapy conference. There are five of you in the group, and only one does psychotherapy. During the conference, you and your group are chatting with some of the psychotherapists from the conference, and it is in this context that you come up with what seems like a new idea for you. Having listened to a few panels, symposia and main speakers, you wonder whether perhaps meditation can accomplish some of what you believe psychotherapy seeks to accomplish, and can be relatively explicit about what those changes are, what those goals are. Here is an apparently new idea that you, your group and the psychotherapists talk about with genuine interest. The idea flowered only when you attended the conference, even though the general idea was somehow floating around outside the crowd of psychotherapists and inside the context of people whose lives included meditation.

As you participate more in the conference on psychotherapy, you get a second wave of creative new ideas. After one set of presentations by psychotherapists, you and your group of meditators are again talking with a group of psychotherapists, and you raise a few issues. Here is one: you say, 'According to what I heard at the conference, psychotherapy has a start and a finish, maybe after 10 or 20 sessions or so, maybe much longer, and most clients then go the rest of their lives without having more sessions of psychotherapy. In meditation, we have sessions every day throughout our lives. The idea is that maybe people can have psychotherapy sessions throughout their entire lives, regularly, maybe once a year or so. Is there some law against this?' The answer is that this may well be a creative new idea, and it comes from offering an idea that is common and accepted outside the crowd but is novel and perhaps even creative when the context is inside the crowd.

Here is another way in which your common way of thinking can yield a new idea within the context of the psychotherapy conference. You say, 'It seems that just about everyone here at the conference presumes that psychotherapy includes a psychotherapist and a patient or client. In meditation, the practitioner carries out meditation by him/herself. Could it be that what you call patients or clients could do "psychotherapy" by themselves? I mean that in the actual session there is just the "practitioner", no "psychotherapist" and "patient" or "client"?' (cf. Mahrer, 2002a)

Here is yet another way in which what seems common in your group may well be a somewhat creative new idea in the field of psychotherapy. You say, 'In meditation, the student learns from the teacher so that the student can become increasingly proficient in their own meditative sessions. Is it sensible that the psychotherapist can be a teacher who has teaching sessions aimed at showing the patient or client how to carry out their own psychotherapy sessions with greater and greater proficiency?'

Whether you come from a group of meditators or surgeons or a soccer team or a string quartet, there are usually some ways of doing things that are commonplace and taken for granted. These are guidelines, practices, rules, ideas, notions. Rather than switching over to the world of psychotherapy, if you enter the crowd of psychotherapists as an outsider, some of your 'outside' guidelines, practices, rules, ideas, notions can give rise to creative new ideas in the field of psychotherapy.

In general, if you are living and being inside the crowd, you may be able to come up with new ideas by going outside the crowd. If you are essentially living and being outside the crowd, you may be able to get new ideas by going inside the crowd. The next step is up to you. You can, if you are inclined to, try out the way that applies to you.

CHAPTER 3

Adopt a Creative New Perspective on the Field of Psychotherapy

I am not talking about moving from your own theory or approach or orientation to some other one. I am not talking about a cognitive therapist moving to a solution focused approach, or a logotherapist adopting a Jungian outlook, or a behaviorist becoming a constructivist therapist, or your moving from a psychodynamic approach to a psychobiological approach.

Instead, I am talking about particular perspectives that may be referred to as 'creative new perspectives' on the field of psychotherapy. They are creative in that they are designed to yield creative new ideas. If you know about these perspectives, if you are able to adopt and to use these new perspectives, the chances are fairly good that you will be able to come up with creative new ideas. That is what they are designed to provide.

These creative new perspectives are ways of seeing and making new sense of the whole field of psychotherapy itself. They can offer a new perspective on what is called psychotherapeutic theorizing or researching or practicing or educating/training. In this sense, these creative new perspectives are different from a cognitive approach or a social learning approach or any other of the relatively common approaches and perspectives in the field of psychotherapy. In other words, rather than merely being yet another perspective 'in' the field of psychotherapy, these are creative new perspectives 'on' the field of psychotherapy.

What do I mean by 'creative new perspectives on the field of psychotherapy'? What are some examples? This chapter will introduce seven ways of seeing the field, each of which can be helpful in arriving at creative new ideas:

(1) See the field in terms of 'models of usefulness' rather than the much more common 'theories of truth'.
(2) See 'exceptions' as doorways to creative new ideas rather than as throwaway exceptions to a general rule or a general principle.
(3) See the field as consisting of 'foundational beliefs'.
(4) See the field as answers to 'basic questions'.
(5) See the field in terms of 'grand cosmologies'.
(6) See the underlying basis of conceptual approaches with high 'challenge and threat value'.
(7) See the alternative 'discovery-oriented approach' to research.

It is my strong impression that precious few psychotherapists are familiar with and know about these creative new perspectives, and it is the exceptionally rare psychotherapist who actually adopts and uses these creative new perspectives. They are essentially absent in the ordinary teaching and training programs of psychotherapy. There is essentially no substantive literature on these creative new perspectives. It seems fairly safe to say that these creative new perspectives are essentially an unknown item in the field of psychotherapy, and this applies to psychotherapy theory, practice, research and education/ training. And yet they can be a precious avenue toward coming up with creative new ideas in the field of psychotherapy.

Many other fields are relatively familiar with these creative new perspectives. In contrast, the field of psychotherapy is relatively unfamiliar with them. Philosophers of science are quite familiar with these creative new perspectives. The field of psychotherapy seems relatively unfamiliar with this literature and with the creative new perspectives it offers.

There are at least three steps that can be taken in order to come up with new ideas by means of these creative new perspectives. The first step is to learn about these creative new perspectives. Study the literature, especially the relevant parts of philosophy of science. The second step is to adopt these creative new perspectives. See what it is like to adopt them, to try them out, to see what they can be like in actual operation. The third step is to use these creative new perspectives to come up with creative new ideas in the field of psychotherapy.

What follow are seven creative new perspectives. The invitation is for some interested psychotherapists to use them to help them to come up with creative new ideas.

1. Adopt and use 'models of usefulness' rather than the common 'theories of truth'

With virtually no notable exception, the field of psychotherapy has fully embraced what may be termed 'theories of truth'. The field has adopted theories of truth almost without question, almost universally, and almost without knowing about the existence of an alternative which may be called 'models of usefulness' (Mahrer, 2004b). This wholesale adoption of theories of truth applies to psychotherapeutic practice, research, education/training and, of course, theory.

My aim is to offer a brief introduction to what may be called theories of truth and models of usefulness, to highlight some major differences between the two, and to make a case that one way of coming up with creative new ideas is by adopting and using models of usefulness.

The odds against even slight success are very high because almost all psychotherapists are devout proponents of theories of truth, because theories of truth have been the solid foundation of the field almost forever, because models of usefulness are essentially unknown strangers from an alien other world, and because there is no track record of creative new ideas coming from psychotherapists letting go of their theories of truth and adopting models of usefulness. Hopefully, there can be an occasional reader who will adopt and use this way of coming up with creative new ideas.

There are at least three main ways in which models of usefulness differ from commonplace theories of truth (Mahrer, 2000b, 2001a, 2004b). These differences are matters of emphasis rather than clean-cut, non-overlapping differences, yet the differences are sharp, relatively easy to recognize, and they make for differences that are significant and serious, one being that models of usefulness are much better for producing creative new ideas.

Here are three ways in which the virtually universal theories of truth differ from models of usefulness, with the latter being essentially missing from the field of psychotherapy, with the exception of an experiential conceptual model (Mahrer, 1989, 1996/2004) and a very few others:

(a) Theories of truth are to be true; models of usefulness are to be useful. For theories of truth, the premium is on framing truths that get at and approximate the true nature of things. For models of usefulness, the premium is on their being helpful in accomplishing some valued aim, goal, purpose, use.

Theories of truth are to get at and to tell the truth about things, to get as close as possible to the real truth, to provide the best approximation of truth, to depict the true state of affairs of reality, to tell what things are really like. According to the way theories of truth see the world, 'The world exists independently of us as knowers, and is the way it is independently of our theoretical knowledge of it. True theories correctly describe that reality' (Chalmers, 1982: 147).

Models of usefulness are the new kid on the block. Their premium is on usefulness. Their justification is mainly that they are useful. They are helpful for some particular job, for achieving some valued, sought-after goal, end, task, use. A 'model is treated as an approximation useful for certain purposes' (Achinstein, 1965: 104). The main way of seeing whether a model of usefulness is any good is by seeing whether it is indeed useful, helpful for the designated job, task, use.

A theory of truth invites testing to see whether it is true, whether what it proclaims is true is really true or not. Go ahead and test the truth of the theory of truth. Check whether what it hypothesizes as true is confirmed or unconfirmed as true, is wrong, is shown to be false. A model of usefulness is tested by seeing whether it is useful, whether it helps to achieve the goal or use.

(b) Both the theory as a whole and its component parts are to be real and true. In contrast, both the model as a whole and its component parts are convenient fictions, useful fictions that are unreal, invented, made up, imaginary.

For theories of truth, its components and parts are real and true. There really are things like egos, metacognitions, growth forces, effectance motivations, developmental stages, paranoia and schizophrenia, defense mechanisms and proactive inhibitions, primary emotions, basic needs for sex and aggression, borderline conditions, and all the other conceptual and personality components and parts. In psychoanalytic theory, there really is something called an unconscious. In cognitive theory, there really are things called cognitions. They are real and true.

As far as models of usefulness are concerned, their components and parts are merely convenient fictions, convenient in that they are useful, fictions in that they are flagrantly imaginary, make-believe, fictitious, unreal. In an experiential model, there are parts called 'potentials for experiencing', and they are merely convenient fictions, not to be found in the bloodstream or the brain, not at all real, merely wholesale inventions. The parts of a model are all convenient fictions. 'They are not … to be proved or disproved, but are convenient representations of things' (Skinner, 1938: 44), convenient in that inventing these parts is helpful in fulfilling the use you have in mind (cf. Rotgers, 1988; van Fraassen, 1980, 1989).

(c) Theories of truth believe in a single underlying truth, which the theories can get at, can know, can approximate. Theories of truth can say, 'That is the way the truth is, that is the truth of things.' Models of usefulness believe in events which are open to alternative modes of construction and representation. Models can say, 'Here is one way of conceptualizing things.'

Theories of truth know that there is a single underlying order and structure to nature, that there is a way that reality is, that there are knowable principles and laws and truths. Theories of truth strive to get as close as possible to the single underlying truth of the way things really and truly are.

Models of usefulness believe that there can be events, phenomena, things, and what they are is marvelously open to alternative modes of description, understanding, representation, construction. That event may be described as white, ceramic or a cup. Not only are these terms or words different from the event they refer to, but these descriptions are likely to differ in their relative usefulness for whatever aim, end, purpose or use the person has in mind.

I hope that a distinction has been made between what may be called theories of truth and models of usefulness, and that the case is sufficient for most readers to appreciate that perhaps the field of psychotherapy is virtually a country of theories of truth, rather than models of usefulness.

1.1 To produce creative new ideas, models of usefulness are better than theories of truth

There are at least four ways in which models of usefulness are perhaps more likely to be cordial to coming up with creative new ideas:

(a) Because of their mission, theories of truth would much more probably be inclined to question and to be skeptical about creative new ideas. Theories of truth would be inclined to ask, 'Is it true?' and 'Does it fit in with what is known, with established knowledge?' In contrast, models of usefulness are relatively free of such constraints. Models are more concerned with whether some idea, including some creative new idea, helps get the job done, and less concerned with whether the creative new idea has to be checked against whatever is considered the base of established knowledge (Duhem, 1996).

When you are able to appreciate the differences between emphasizing whether something is true or emphasizing whether it is useful, you are almost pushed into having creative new ideas. Suppose that you appreciate that the thing over there can be described, with equal truth, as white, ceramic or a cup, but that calling it a cup is much more useful when you are thirsty. Suppose that you want to find a shoe repair shop, and two strangers tell you things that are equally true, but unequal in usefulness. One says, 'There is a shoe repair shop in this town,' and the other says, 'There is a shoe repair shop at 140 Queen Street, which is two streets ahead; turn right and it is the second shop.' You have a creative new idea along these lines: two statements or propositions may be equal in truth, but unequal in usefulness. See for yourself how this creative new idea may be formulated so as to apply to, and perhaps make a creative difference in regard to, the testing of research hypotheses. This is one way that models of usefulness can be superior to theories of truth in helping you to come up with creative new ideas.

(b) Because models are created to help get some job done, they can be, by nature, much more imaginative, silly, unrealistic, whimsical, playful, fantasy-like. The criterion is whether or not it works, rather than whether it is true. The net result is that models of usefulness can be the playground for creative new ideas.

Models are cordial to pictorial representations of how things may be depicted in order to get some job done. Accordingly, the generated pictures can be delightfully primitive or highly sophisticated. They can be utterly fictitious or uncannily accurate. They can have little or nothing to do with the way things really are, or they can be eerily predictive of the way things will be found to be. Models are free to be fabulously creative because they are wholly free of all constraints except one: they must be helpful in the practical job to be done.

A woman I knew had asked me to please check on her place while she was out of town, and I was beginning to be frustrated because the key did not open her front door. That was when I heard the earnest voice of the little girl who had come up the steps: 'Do you know how keys work?' I was fumbling both with the key and with the beginnings of an answer that had something to do with tumblers, cams and cylinders, and I heard myself simply saying, 'Uh ... not really.' She explained carefully and slowly that the key has to tickle the lock because locks unlock when they are tickled and start giggling, and that is what the key is for. 'How do I tickle the lock?' She explained simply: 'Wiggle it.' I wiggled the key and the door opened. A few days later, I was again at the door with the key, and of course I pictured how the key tickled the lock, so of course I jiggled and wiggled the inserted key and of course the door opened. Her model worked. I could almost hear the lock giggling. I could feel the joy of a creative picture, a model.

(c) Models are joyously welcoming of major modification and wholesale replacement by better ones. If one doesn't work, be creative. Invent a better one. There are always better models waiting in the wings. All it takes is a puff of creativity. Creativity is the theme song of models of usefulness.

There is no law that you should cling to a model whether or not it works. Models are refreshingly not at all heavily saturnine, locked into a fixed place, entrenched, anchored in a solid foundation. Models do not demand dedication or devotion, eternal respect and worship. Replacement by better models is not apologized for as inconsistency, but welcomed as a flexible willingness to adopt better and more useful helpers. Models are wellsprings of creativity.

(d) The closer theories of truth come to doing a good job of approximating the truth, the less room there is for creative new ideas. Suppose that we become reasonably satisfied that we have been successful in knowing what the primary emotions are, what the ingredients are of an effective therapist–client relationship, what to assess and evaluate in initial sessions. If we think in terms of theories of truth, we now just about know the truth. Creative speculation, having new ideas, may as well turn to the next matter because we know the truth about primary emotions, the ingredients of effective therapist–client relationships, or what to assess and evaluate in initial sessions.

What makes matters even worse, once we know the truth, is that it is so tempting to wrap it in the robes of an eternal truth, a basic canon, a dictum or axiom of truth. Carving it in stone means that creative new ideas may as well find something else to play with. What is the truth about 'causality'? When we assure ourselves that we now know, we elevate what we know into a piece of truth, of reality itself; 'when notions, such as causality, are held to be the only possible views, it is but a short step to elevating those views to the status of reality itself' (Slife and Williams, 1995: 97).

In contrast, models of usefulness are essentially born and bred to invite creative new ideas. Instead of saying, 'All right, now we know most of what is to be known about that,' models of usefulness are more inclined to keep asking, 'Can you come up with a still more useful model that can be still more useful?'

Models of usefulness are conceived and designed to be superior to theories of truth in enabling the psychotherapy theorist, researcher, practitioner or teacher/trainer to come up with creative new ideas. In terms of creativity, the case is that models are more curious, explorative, discovery-oriented, adventuresome, audacious, bold, and much more helpful in coming up with what is new and creative. If you are drawn toward coming up with creative new ideas, the invitation is to welcome and embrace models of usefulness rather than theories of truth.

2. Use exceptions as exceptional doorways to creative new ideas, rather than as exceptions to a general rule

The most common perspective tends to think in terms of general rules, general principles, general truths. In this common way of looking at things, it is acknowledged that the rules and principles and truths are not perfect. Of course there will be exceptions. That is to be expected. That is why the common perspective frames general rules and principles and truths by using words and phrases such as 'in general', 'normally', 'in most cases', 'under most conditions'. Exceptions are expected exceptions, mere exceptions, a little noise in the system of rules and principles and truths. You can hardly expect the rule to apply in every instance. When the common perspective sees things in terms of general rules, principles and truths, everything remains in order as long as the number of exceptions is small enough to be unthreatening to the statistics.

This is the way the world tends to look from the common perspective. Exceptions have meaning mainly in terms of their threat value to the general rule or principle or truth. A few little exceptions don't hurt much. The idea of 'creative new ideas' does not come into play much.

But there is a qualitatively different perspective on the meaning and on the value of exceptions. From this altogether different perspective, exceptions can be exceptional doorways to creative new ideas. Where the common perspective says, 'Look at that distribution!', the other perspective says, 'Look at those wonderful exceptions!' Where the common perspective says, 'I found a general rule, principle, truth!', the other perspective says, 'I found a jewel of an exception!' A perspective that searches out valued and impressive exceptions is superior to a perspective that searches for general rules, principles and truths in coming up with creative new ideas.

The history of physics seems to have plenty of dramatic examples of how creative new ideas could spring from a perspective that kept an excited eye on exciting exceptions to general rules, principles, truths, laws.

> It is because a piece of amber rubbed with silk placed the laws of gravity in error that physics created the laws of electrostatics. It is because a

magnet produced effects contrary to these same laws of gravity that physics imagined the laws of magnetism. It is because Oersted found an exception to the laws of electrostatics and magnetism that Ampere invented the laws of electrodynamics and electromagnetism. (Duhem, 1996: 108)

By having and using this alternative perspective, the field of physics was open to creative new ideas. The field of psychotherapy can follow suit by holding to this alternative perspective of valuing exceptional exceptions to the general rules, principles and truths.

In the common perspective, if 99 out of 100 cases conform to the general rule, you are justified in paying little or no attention to the single exception. In the alternative perspective, it may very well be the one exception that opens the door to the creative new idea. If 99 of the dead bodies remain dead when the special music is played, the new perspective allows you to be excited about the one person who comes to life and tells you about what it was like to have been dead. If the incantation of the monk had no effect on the terminal cancer of 99 patients, the alternative perspective justifies your being creatively excited by the one exception whose terminal cancer vanished forever. If the single session had no apparent effect on 99 of the cases, the new perspective holds you by the hand and ushers you into the world of creative new ideas by studying the one exception where the person seemed to undergo a wholesale transformation into becoming a qualitatively whole new person. Creative new ideas are the gift of a perspective that flags the exceptional exceptions.

In studying approximately 500 sessions of about 80 master psychotherapists, my research team and I explicitly adopted a perspective of searching out those special moments on the tapes where we were impressed with the impressive exceptions, the unusual and atypical exceptions that seemed special, compelling, wonderful. In studying each practitioner, it was easy to appreciate the way the practitioner did therapy, the principles that seemed to guide the practitioner throughout the session. But that was not what our perspective flagged. Instead, we were on the lookout for the extraordinary, the unusual special changes that opened the doors to creative new ideas about psychotherapy. It was this alternative perspective that allowed us to find and to follow that exceptional exception into the magical world of creative new ideas, into what may be termed a 'discovery-oriented approach' to psychotherapy research (Mahrer, 1985, 1988, 1996a, 1996b, 2003, 2004a; Mahrer and Boulet, 1999).

3. When you can see the field as consisting of 'foundational beliefs', then you can create new and better foundational beliefs

You can get creative new ideas by adopting a creative new perspective in which you see the field as consisting of what may be called 'foundational beliefs'. When you are able to adopt this way of seeing the field, then you can get creative new ideas by creating new and better foundational beliefs.

This means first explaining what foundational beliefs are, and how this way of seeing the field differs from the much more common way of seeing the field.

3.1 Here is a meaning of 'foundational beliefs'
In the field of psychotherapy, 'foundational beliefs' can be taken as basic propositions that are accepted as true, as basic truths, as the basic principles, the cornerstones on which the field rests, the fundamental givens, the notions and ideas that are taken as foundational, fundamental, true. Foundational beliefs share much of the spirit of what, in some other fields, is there in such technically different words and phrases as postulates, theorems, axioms, dictums, canons.

If there were a cumulative body of psychotherapeutic knowledge, a part of the contents would probably be these foundational beliefs.

3.2 Most psychotherapists do not have an especially clear picture of their foundational beliefs
There are virtually no lists of what may be taken as 'foundational beliefs' in the field of psychotherapy. It is hard to find relatively formal, comprehensive, generally accepted lists either for the field as a whole or for given perspectives or approaches.

Furthermore, a case can be built that there are identifiable ways that the field has hidden these foundational beliefs, kept them concealed, unexplicated, unspecified (Chalmers, 1982; Feigl, 1953; Fodor, 1987; Kagan, 1996; Kantor, 1945; Mahrer, 1998, 2000b; Mays, 1977; Slife and Williams, 1995). It is as if the field of psychotherapy has built itself a profession and a science resting on a set of foundational beliefs of which the field is largely unaware.

One way the field keeps itself from knowing its own foundational beliefs is simply by having no public lists of its foundational beliefs (Mahrer, 1999, 2003). In return, because there are no public lists, foundational beliefs tend to be even more hidden and concealed. The net result is that most psychotherapists have little or no idea what their foundational beliefs are, and little or no idea that they have little or no idea what their foundational beliefs are.

Second, foundational beliefs can be concealed inside standard vocabulary and standard practices (Slife and Williams, 1995; Whitehead, 1929). Imagine the sets of foundational beliefs you have quietly accepted if you do an intake assessment that includes a neurological examination of the patient's presenting symptoms. Imagine the foundational beliefs you have allowed into your way of thinking when you are discussing how the patient learned her behavior by means of 'conditioned responses'. Imagine the foundational beliefs you have bought by accepting that the patient has a borderline condition.

Third, foundational beliefs can be concealed by studying all sorts of things 'about' the foundational belief while discretely avoiding the foundational belief itself. A foundational belief in schizophrenia can be made both alive and concealed, vibrant and hidden, by studying the course of the illness, the kinds and types, the symptoms, the treatment, the epidemiology, the demographics, the cultural effects, while never focusing on the foundational belief of schizophrenia itself.

Fourth, neighboring foundational beliefs protect and conceal one another so that the unsuspecting inquirer is easily confused and lost in a labyrinth of mirrors (Chalmers, 1982; Mahrer, 2000b). When you believe you are headed toward a foundational belief that therapeutic change is a function of insight and understanding of childhood experiences, you can be deflected by a neighboring foundational belief that childhood experiences determine adult functioning.

Fifth, almost everyone grows up with deep-seated 'folk psychologies' containing all sorts of foundational beliefs (Fodor, 1987; Furnham, 1987; Kagan, 1996; Stich, 1983; Valentine, 1996) that have probably remained safely hidden and concealed throughout one's lifetime. Students can arrive for training, go through training and graduate from training with little or no awareness of the foundational beliefs tucked inside their hidden and concealed folk psychologies.

Sixth, the foundational beliefs of the reigning conceptual system tend to become (a) increasingly presumed and assumed, and (b) increasingly concealed and hidden. It is as if the more prevalent is the regnant, popular, mainstream approach, the more its proponents embrace its foundational beliefs, and the more sealed off and barricaded are the foundational beliefs from inquiry and examination. It is as if the crowd brainwashes itself.

Seventh, punish those who seek to inquire into the foundational beliefs. Foundational beliefs are safely concealed by a protective warning: thou shall not inquire into the hallowed foundational beliefs. Even if the inquirer dares to question the injunction, consider the questioning a violation and prepare the punishment.

Of course you can live in a state of not having a reasonably clear picture of the foundational beliefs in the field. You can collude in hiding them, without publicly announcing that you are colluding in hiding them. Or you can work to get a clear picture of the field's foundational beliefs, and you can go further by using some helpful guidelines to create your own foundational beliefs.

3.3 Here are some examples of foundational beliefs

These examples are taken from an amateur provisional attempt to identify 75 'foundational beliefs' in the field of psychotherapy (Mahrer, 2003; cf. Mahrer, 1995, 2000b, 2004b). None of these are 'official'. They may or may not have general acceptance, though each was taken from a wide distribution of authoritative texts. Some of these are more 'foundational' than others.

- There is a cumulative body of psychotherapeutic knowledge; research is a primary gatekeeper for what is admitted into or withdrawn from the cumulative body of knowledge.
- Prediction and explanation of empirically validated facts are important criteria for judging the worth of theories of psychotherapy.
- Theories of psychotherapy are judged, examined and tested by deriving hypotheses that are subjected to scientific verification, confirmation, disconfirmation, refutation and falsification.
- The outcomes of psychotherapy can be rigorously assessed as successful, effective, beneficial, or not so, essentially apart from philosophical value systems.
- Biological, neurological, physiological and chemical events and variables are basic to psychological events and variables.
- The brain is a basic determinant of human behavior.
- Human beings have inborn, intrinsic, biological and psychological needs, drives, instincts and motivations; these include needs and drives for survival, sex, aggression, object-seeking, contact-comfort.
- There are biopsychological stages of human growth and development.
- Responses followed by satisfying consequences tend to be strengthened; responses followed by unsatisfying consequences tend to be weakened.
- There are mental illnesses, diseases and disorders.
- Clients seek psychotherapy for, and psychotherapy is treatment of, psychological-psychiatric problems, distress, mental disorders, personal difficulties, and problems in living.
- The practitioner initially assesses and diagnoses the problem or mental disorder, and then selects and applies the appropriate treatment.

- The therapist–client relationship is prerequisite to successful psycho-therapy.
- Insight and understanding are prerequisite to successful psychotherapy.
- There are differential treatments of choice for differential psychological problems and mental disorders.
- Most psychotherapeutic theories and approaches can be rigorously identified and differentiated from one another.
- Single approaches may be combined or integrated into a larger frame-work that is superior to any component approach.

3.4 Follow these guidelines to start from foundational beliefs, and to arrive at creative new ideas

All the guidelines depend on your having some place to start.

(a) You are welcome to start with my provisional list of 75 foundational beliefs (Mahrer, 2003). This list is for and from the general field of psychotherapy, rather than any particular approach, and it includes foundational beliefs having to do with psychotherapy theory, research, practice and training.

If you prefer, you can start with texts that try to set forth the basic ideas, the canons, the dictums, the fundamental truths, the starting points, whatever is taken for granted in your own part of the field. Look for authoritative texts setting out the foundational beliefs in cognitive behavioral therapy, or in psychoanalytic theory, or the fundamental principles underlying psychotherapy research.

It can take some work to find what you think of as a foundational belief. Once you locate it, try to put it in a form that is reasonably explicit, perhaps a little more carefully worded. For example, you may find a statement that generally refers to insight as an important factor in psychotherapy. Start here and then try to put this general idea in a form that is more explicit, more carefully worded. Are you thinking of insight in some narrow specialized sense or more generally? Do you think of insight as important or merely helpful, as a necessary condition or as actually necessary and sufficient? What is it supposed to be important for? In any case, is your proposition to cut across various approaches, or is it restricted to just a few approaches?

Taking account of these kinds of questions and considerations, coming up with an explicit foundational belief can be difficult, and it can also be a creative enterprise (cf. Ariew and Barker, 1996) that culminates in this explicitly stated foundational belief: insight and understanding are prerequisite to successful psychotherapy.

Whether you start with my list or your own careful reading, you have a foundational belief to look at. This is where you start.

(b) If the foundational belief is acceptable to you, pass it by. You are not likely to come up with creative new ideas if the foundational belief is already satisfactory.

(c) Find a foundational belief that seems somewhat acceptable but needs a nip here and a tuck there, a change here and there, a clause deleted or altered or added. It has to be changed in order to be acceptable, but it is reasonably close as it is.

For example, suppose that this is your reaction to these foundational beliefs: 'There are biopsychological stages of human growth and development' and 'The practitioner initially assesses and diagnoses the problem or mental disorder, and then selects and applies the appropriate treatment.' You are engaging in creative thinking, coming up with new ideas, when you figure out how the foundational beliefs would have to be revised, altered, modified to be acceptable to you. Go ahead and revise, alter, modify until the statement meets with your approval (Bartley, 1984, 1988; Radnitsky, 1988). You have come up with a creative new idea.

(d) Suppose that you find the whole foundational belief to be unacceptable to you. It can't be made acceptable by a few changes here and there. You decline the entire foundational belief. You may object to the key terms and phrases. For example, there is no place in your thinking for 'biopsychological stages of human growth and development' or for something called 'mental disorders'. Or you may seriously object to the very idea of there being biopsychological stages of human growth and development, or that the main aim in initial sessions is to diagnose the problem and then select and apply the appropriate treatment. The whole idea of the foundational belief is objectionable, ill-fitting, not to your taste.

Here is the opportunity for you to come up with a creative idea. First of all, do not simply decline or reject the foundational belief. Do not say, 'I decline or reject that foundational belief. I do not believe in that foundational belief. That foundational belief is not a part of my way of thinking.' Instead, you are entering into creative new thinking by searching for your own winning alternative, for a foundational belief that you can happily accept, for your own pleasing alternative. The searching for an acceptable alternative is the creative act. Arriving at a satisfying alternative is coming up with a new idea.

If you wholeheartedly reject the idea that there are biopsychological stages of human growth and development, then you may be facing some deep issues, and, if so, what are your positions on those deep issues? How does a person become the person that the person becomes? Are there 'things' inside an infant altogether different from and much more important than whatever leads to biopsychological stages of growth and development? If you reject the idea of stages of human growth and development, then what is your alternative belief? These are the kinds of questions that can spur you into the arena of creative new ideas.

If you wholeheartedly reject that the practitioner initially assesses and diagnoses the problem or mental disorder, and then selects and applies the appropriate treatment, then what does the practitioner do in initial sessions? You are already in the arena of creative new ideas. What you come up with can very well be a creative new idea.

Your preferred alternative may be your creative new idea. It may be similar to or different from my own preferred alternative. Check out my preferred alternative for virtually each of the 75 foundational beliefs on my list (Mahrer, 2003). Your preferred alternative may be the alternative of choice of client-centered therapists or behavior therapists or some other established constituency. Or your preferred alternative may be a new creative alternative for the field.

(e) Suppose that you decline virtually all of the foundational beliefs that seem common and traditional in the field. Suppose that your own alternative foundational beliefs do not correspond to those of any smaller constituency, such as a rogue neo-psychoanalytic group or an archaic behavioral group or some other known group. One possibility is that your own foundational beliefs are simply unusual, highly uncommon, idiosyncratic. Another possibility is that your general outlook and framework, your own foundational beliefs, are not only uncommon and unusual but also possess that special quality of being preciously creative.

In any case, you started by being able to see the field as consisting of foundational beliefs, and then you used the suggested guidelines to come up with your own creative new ideas, your own foundational beliefs.

3.5 Starting from generally accepted foundational beliefs, invent a creative new perspective on the field of psychotherapy

You are invited to play a game of coming up with, building and inventing, a creative new perspective on the field of psychotherapy. The game consists of a number of steps.

1. The first step is to start with some foundational beliefs that are generally accepted in the field of psychotherapy. Look for some basic ideas that are

almost unquestioned in the field, that are generally taken for granted. They are exemplified in the major, popular, dominant approaches, whatever approaches are fashionable at the time. Start with my list (Mahrer, 2003) if that is handy.

2. The second step is to put on a creative cap and to come up with a creative alternative foundational belief for each one that you study. Start with one foundational belief, come up with a creative alternative, then proceed to a second foundational belief. Aim at a small number, for example, four to six or so.

    Follow the guidelines described earlier. Let yourself be creative enough to come up with alternatives that can violate the generally accepted foundational belief, that can set them aside. Be as creative as you can. Be bold. Go far beyond the usual constraints of reality, or of having to have a way of defending what you come up with. Your alternative need not make good sense, or have a small constituency that favors it, or have roots in the writings of some great thinkers.

3. When you have a small number of alternative foundational beliefs, perhaps four to six or so, put on your creative cap again and see if you can use these foundational beliefs to invent a creative new perspective on the field of psychotherapy. Let yourself be willing to steer clear of most of the perspectives that are floating around in the larger field of psychotherapy, quite aside from the more popular, dominant perspectives. You are allowing these four to six alternative foundational beliefs to generate their own creative new perspective that is a creative new departure from the perspectives that are so well-known, well-accepted in the field.

Here are some foundational beliefs. Suppose that they are relatively common, generally accepted in the field of psychotherapy. Each is followed by what can happen when you follow the guidelines and search for your own creative alternative:

- Biological, neurological and physiological events and variables are basic to psychological events and variables.
    Psychological events and variables are essentially independent of and not reducible to biological, neurological and physiological events and variables.
- Human beings have basic potentialities for being. These have essentially none of the properties of biological and psychological needs and drives.
- Pain is aversive; behavior tends to reduce, avoid or eliminate pain.
    Behavior is a means of helping to bring about a state of being that is

60

important for the particular person. The state of being may be painful or pleasurable. Accordingly, behavior can reduce, avoid or eliminate pain, or behavior can enhance, create, heighten or deepen pain, turmoil, distress, unhappiness, anguish.

• There are mental illnesses, diseases and disorders.

The notion of mental illnesses, diseases and disorders is limited to conceptual systems that have a place for, that make conceptual sense of, that include the concepts that accompany and go with the notion of mental illnesses, diseases and disorders. Not all conceptual systems necessarily include the notion of mental illnesses, diseases and disorders.

• Insight and understanding are prerequisite to significant psychotherapeutic change.

Insight and understanding can be one of a number of consequences of significant psychotherapeutic change.

These are five perhaps common foundational beliefs, each one followed by a creative alternative that can come about when a person follows the suggested guidelines. The creative challenge is to start with these five alternative foundational beliefs and allow them to grow into a wholesale, large-scale, creative new perspective on the field of psychotherapy. There can be a social learning perspective, a cognitive perspective, an existential perspective, a psychodynamic perspective, perhaps one or two more, and your own creative new perspective evolving from the five alternative foundational beliefs. Are you ready and willing to play the creative game? See how ready and willing you are to come up with a whole new perspective on the field of psychotherapy, a creative new perspective.

4. When you can see the field as mainly answers to 'basic questions', you can come up with creative new ideas as you look for better and better answers

First you must be able to see the field as mainly answers to 'basic questions'. For most psychotherapists, this is a big switch, a quantum switch. It doesn't mean that the field really and truly consists of answers to basic questions. It only means that you are able to play a mind-game in which you are able to see the field as mainly answers to basic questions.

Then you must be able to see how important it is to keep looking for better and better answers to these basic questions. You must be able to see that one way of advancing the field of psychotherapy is by looking for and finding these better and better answers to the basic questions.

Looking for better and better answers is essentially coming up with creative new ideas. In other words, the search for better and better answers is virtually the same as the search for creative new ideas.

4.1 Think in terms of 'alternative' answers and 'better' answers, rather than a 'right' answer

You can think in terms of a 'right' answer to a question. You can also think of continually better and better answers to some questions (Mahrer, 2004b), and that means accepting some ways of acknowledging an answer as 'better'. It can be better in terms of some end or goal or use that you have in mind so that this answer is better because it is more useful in helping you to achieve the end you have in mind. It may be better because it opens up whole new possibilities, or because it is simpler, cleaner. Whatever the reason, coming up with creative new ideas is helped by thinking in terms of better and better answers to basic questions, rather than thinking in terms of finding the right answer to the basic question.

Coming up with creative new ideas can also be helped by thinking of alternative answers to basic questions, rather than finding the single right answer. Of course there are questions that can have an apparently right answer, or one that comes close. Here are a few: what is the square root of 1929? what is the speed of light? what is the circumference of the earth? what is the chemical content of the water in this glass?

In the field of psychotherapy, each approach, such as cognitive theory, psychodynamic theory or social learning theory, likes to think that its answer is the right answer. If you rise above the various approaches, or if you look across the various approaches, the picture is of a set of alternative answers rather than a single right answer.

If we look back over the history of dominant approaches, each period has had its dominant approach's single right answer to the basic question. Starting a few thousand years ago, each period has had its fashionably right answer to basic questions such as these: what accounts for a person becoming bizarre, demented, losing their mind, going insane? what are the origins of what is called 'personality,' the characteristic way that a given person is? what accounts for dreams? The historical view gives a picture of succeeding waves of alternative answers to basic questions, rather than an answer that essentially closes off the search for the right answer.

In the field of psychotherapy, basic questions can be thought of as having alternative answers, and this picture leaves room for better and better answers. But first you must be able to see the field as mainly answers to basic questions, and this means you must have a fairly clear picture of what is meant by basic questions.

4.2 Here is what is meant by basic questions

There are at least four kinds of questions that may be regarded as 'basic'.

(a) Basic questions can include those that have been there for millennia, and have a long history of fashionable answers. For perhaps the last two thousand years or so, since long before there was a formal profession or science of psychotherapy, there have been some basic questions that have begged for answers from great thinkers in fields such as philosophy and theology, politics and literature, many of the arts and sciences. Here are some examples. How did I become the person I am? What were the basic origins of the person I am? Why do I act and behave the way I act and behave? How and why do I have such troubles and worries, pains and sufferings, distresses and dreads? Can there be significant change in the person I am? How can I become more of the person I would like to become? How can I become a person who is happier, more joyful, more buoyant, more at peace with myself? How can I be free of my own troubles and worries, pains and sufferings, distresses and dreads? Why is it that some people seem to go crazy, lose their minds, do such weird and bizarre things? Where do dreams come from and what do they mean? How can people get along with one another in peace and happiness rather than with such hatred and unhappiness? What is the good life, the ideal or optimal way of being?

(b) Basic questions can include what may be called the 'great unanswered questions' in the field as a whole, or for some particular approach, or for a given psychotherapist. These refer to the burning questions, the vexing and compelling questions, the questions that challenge and drive the psychotherapist to try to answer them. Great unanswered questions may have a long history of being the epic questions, the profound questions such as these from other fields: is there life elsewhere in the universe? is there intelligent life elsewhere in the universe? how did the universe begin? is the universe expanding or shrinking? On the other hand, great unanswered questions may refer to matters that are more practical, technical, applied, such as: how can cold fusion be achieved? how can a dead body be restored to life?

(c) Basic questions can also include questions that may be referred to as 'breakthrough questions'. These are questions whose answers can open the way to major advances in the field, to groundbreaking new developments, to the discovery and opening up of whole new areas (Mahrer, 1997a; Nadler, Hibine and Farrell, 1995). Breakthrough questions are the important questions that are recognized as puzzling, as challengingly unanswered, and this in turn 'depends on our propensity to be puzzled' (Polanyi, 1967: 38). In other fields, historians (e.g. Kuhn, 1959, 1970, 1977; Lakatos, 1963, 1970, 1974) have documented how breakthrough questions have first been recognized as unsolved, and then their answers recognized as answers, enabling great thinkers such as Copernicus and Kepler to answer such breakthrough questions as whether the sun revolved around the earth or the earth revolved around the sun, and whether planetary orbits were or were not perfect circles.

Of course, some basic questions may qualify both as great unanswered questions and as breakthrough questions, and some as one but not the other.

Basic questions have a history of one fashionable answer after another, and of somehow surviving each wave of fashionable answers. The field of psychotherapy can be seen as having a short history of about a century or so, and it can be hard to find convincing evidence of basic questions that have survived a series of fashionable answers. There are some. It is easier to spot a basic question when an historian can trace fashionable answers over a longer period of, for example, 500 years or so.

Whether the history is closer to 100 years or closer to 500 years, each period can claim that it has found the answer. What are the origins of 'personality'? What accounts for a person having 'bad feelings'? How can significant changes occur in the way a person acts and behaves? Each period is entitled to claim that it has found the answer. Each period can claim that its answer has been accepted by its leading theoreticians, researchers, teachers. Each period can elevate its answer into a generally accepted truth, and remove the basic question as a basic question on the grounds that it has been answered.

However, the historian can see that each period's answer has been replaced by the succeeding period's answer, and that each period's answer was solemnly pronounced as the final answer. The historian can see that the career of basic questions is much longer than the career of fashionable answers.

The historian can see that claiming that the field has an answer to the basic question is not necessarily strong evidence, and can be weak evidence, that the basic question is no longer a basic question. And the historian's evidence is the past periods of final answers to the basic question.

The historian can see that the continuous search for better and better answers to basic questions, to the 'truths' of the past and present periods, can be the fuel for creative new ideas. 'Although dependence on the past cannot be denied, progress also occurs because dissatisfaction with the "truths" of yesterday stimulates our search for better answers today' (Millon, 1999: 3).

Coming up with creative new ideas can come from being able to see the field of psychotherapy as consisting of answers to basic questions, and from having a reasonably clear picture of the meaning of 'basic questions'.

4.3 Here are some examples of basic questions

These are largely taken from a longer list of basic questions organized under a number of categories (Mahrer, 2004b). The disclaimer clause is that neither the basic questions nor the categories should be thought of as official or formal or arrived at through some systematic process or procedure. They are strictly armchair, provisional, and offered in the spirit that there aren't many other such lists or categories of basic questions, so here is a first approximation that cheerfully invites improvement.

In this provisional category system, some basic questions are regarded as relating to 'conceptualization'. Here are a few examples. Are biological, neurological, physiological, chemical events and variables basic to psychological events and variables? What are the generally accepted truths, laws and canons in the field of psychotherapy? How can a conceptual system be improved, advanced? What are the sufficient grounds for abandoning a conceptual system? How can conceptual systems be combined or integrated into a new conceptual system? How can a conceptual system be judged as superior to its plausible rivals?

Here are some basic questions having to do with psychotherapy research. What are useful and effective means of advancing psychotherapeutic knowledge? How can research indicate that an hypothesis is wrong, false, refuted? What are the careful, rigorous guidelines for arriving at an hypothesis? What are the careful, rigorous guidelines for modifying a conceptual system on the basis of research findings? What identifies a research hypothesis or question as superior to other research hypotheses or questions?

Here are some basic questions having to do with 'personality'. What are the fundamental origins, the primitive groundwork or beginnings, of personality? What are the components or parts of 'personality structure'? What accounts for the occurrence of behavior? How and why does a person have feelings that are good and pleasant or bad and unpleasant? Can there be substantive change in what may be termed a person's 'basic nature' or foundational way of being? To what extent and in what ways does a person help organize, create, build the person's own personal world?

Here are some examples of basic questions having to do with psychotherapy. What are the purposes, aims and goals of psychotherapy?

What are the criteria, the indications, that psychotherapeutic changes are welcomed, valuable, desirable? What are the inclusive and exclusive defining characteristics of what is regarded as a 'psychotherapy'? What are the underlying dictums, basic principles, laws, canons of psychotherapy? What accounts for therapists and patients or clients seeking out and being with one another? How can new and advanced methods of psychotherapy be developed? What are useful and effective ways for psychotherapy to use past events? How can psychotherapy enable a person to be free of personal pain and anguish, suffering and turmoil?

4.4 Follow these guidelines to come up with creative new ideas

When you are able to see the field as answers to basic questions, there are guidelines you can follow to come up with creative new ideas. Here are some.

Start with a basic question and the commonly accepted answers, and then try to come up with creative new answers to the basic question. Picture a sheet of paper with a basic question at the top, a basic question such as: what accounts for a person seeking out and being with a person designated as a psychotherapist? Picture that the sheet includes one or two or more relatively common and accepted answers. Knowing the basic question and the commonly accepted answers, try to come up with a new answer or two. The emphasis is on a creatively new answer, rather than finding one that may be 'right'.

Are you willing to try? Suppose that we start with this basic question: what are the purposes, aims or goals of psychotherapy? It can be easy to come up with lots of answers, at all sorts of levels of abstraction, and it can be hard to come up with a few generally accepted answers. For the purposes of the game, suppose we start with this answer: 'The purposes, aims and goals of psychotherapy are to treat psychological problems, presenting complaints, symptoms or mental disorders, and to enable patients to restore normal functioning.'

Here is what you are to do: given this answer, put on your creative hat, and try to come up with creative new answers, answers that are not especially common, answers that may be exceedingly uncommon. Go ahead, note down two or three creative answers.

As you think, let yourself enter the realm of answers that depart significantly from the generally accepted, fashionable answers. Enter the realm of answers that are quite different, alien, boldly new. As you think, do not let yourself be blocked by worries that what you are coming up with may not be original, that others may have written extensively about the new idea, that what you are finding is not new at all.

This guideline invites you to keep one eye on the basic question, to keep another eye on the generally accepted, fashionable answers, and then to use these fashionable answers as a point of departure as you throw yourself into the realm of creative new ideas.

The second guideline is to confront the truly 'big' questions in the field of psychotherapy. Confront these questions by putting them front and center, and by doing your best to answer them in creative ways.

These big questions include what may be called the 'great unanswered questions' and the 'breakthrough questions'. Great unanswered questions include the questions that have been around from long before there was a field of professional psychotherapy. There may have been fashionable answers, one after another, but the question remained as one fashionable answer was replaced by another. In other words, the question survived a series of fashionable answers and is still a great unanswered question today. These are the great unanswered questions. They are the burning questions that have been around for a long time and still are great unanswered questions.

Here is a small sample. Do your best to study each great unanswered question and to come up with a creative new answer:

- What is the basic origin of 'personality'? Where does it all come from in the first place? What is the basic foundation for the person that a person is?
- How can we make sense of dreams and dreaming?
- How and why does a person have feelings that are painful, distressing, unhappy?
- How can a person be free of feelings that are painful, distressing, unhappy, especially feelings that seem to have characterized the person throughout their entire life?
- What accounts for a person being in a state that seems alien, bizarre, extraordinary, weird, unusual; deranged, lunatic, crazy, out of one's mind, demented?
- What can a person become? What is an ideal, optimal person like?

In addition to these great unanswered questions, what may be called the big questions can also include breakthrough questions. These are the questions that are generally regarded as essentially not answered. These questions seem to have been around for a long time, challenging the field to provide the answer that can virtually revolutionize the field, advance the field in leaps and bounds, open up whole new areas, take the field to a whole new level (Mahrer, 1997a).

Here is a small sample of these breakthrough questions. You can get the creative juices flowing by focusing on these kinds of questions and doing your best to come up with creative answers:

- What can be done so that a person undergoes wholesale, complete, radical, deep-seated metamorphosis or transformation into a whole new person?
- If this wondrous, transformational change can be brought about, how can it last for a while or forever?
- How can a person achieve what may be regarded as an optimal state, a state of being an ideal person?
- How can a group, community, society achieve a state of peacefulness, tranquility, happiness, joy, with minimal pain, anguish, unhappiness?
- How can one person know, touch and be touched by, undergo, what is occurring deep inside another person?
- How can we reach a person who seems unreachable, make person-to-person contact with a person who seems essentially beyond such contact?

A third guideline is to study a written text by looking for the underlying basic question. As you ordinarily read a paragraph or a page, it is common to read by looking for the main points that the author seems to be making, or to read by seeing what the text has to add to some topic you have in mind, a topic such as assessment measures of therapeutic change in children or the parts of the brain involved in 'false memories'.

Instead, the guideline suggests that you read the paragraph or page to try to identify the underlying basic question that is here, that may be implied. It is as if you ask, 'What is the basic question that is here, that is implied, that is beneath the text?' Finding and clarifying the basic question is usually an act of discovery. You begin by identifying the basic question.

Then you try to put into words what the author's answer seems to be. You have a fairly good idea of the underlying basic question and the author's own answer. Now you are ready for the truly creative part.

Ask yourself, 'If this is the underlying basic question, and if this is the author's own answer, then what is my own, personal, perhaps creative answer?' You might, of course, agree with the author's answer. If you allow yourself to go further, to find your own answer, allow yourself to be a little loose, a little far-fetched, whimsical, far-out, inventive, creative.

Here is an example. The article is about the dreams of people who have been through serious personal tragedies. You concentrate on this particular paragraph or two, and ask yourself what underlying basic question is here. You have to do the work because the author's text talks about what it talks about, rather than focusing on the underlying basic question. When you find the basic question, you formulate it as follows: what accounts for dreams? It is as simple as that.

Now that you have identified an underlying basic question, try to figure out the author's answer. This is easier to figure out. The author's position is that dreams are a way for the person to cope with personal tragedy, significant personal traumas that might have occurred to the person recently or long ago.

You are now ready for some creative thinking. You know the basic question. You know the author's answer. Can you come up with a creative new answer? One way of declining to come up with a creative new answer is to embrace an established answer to the basic question. You can write down that dreams are symbolic expressions of deeper wishes, and that is that. This is not a creative answer; it is reciting a generally accepted answer. Here is the challenge: now that you have a clear formulation of the basic question, the author's answer, and the commonly accepted answer, can you think of a creative new answer, especially if you allow yourself to get a little loose and creative, a little outlandish and free of realistic constraints? Go ahead. Take your time. Think. Here is where you can be wallowing in the possibility of creative new ideas.

Throughout this method, the key is being able to adopt a mind-set in which the field is seen as predominantly answers to basic questions. When you can do this, then creative new ideas can flower as you search for better and better answers to these basic questions.

5. Actively seek a new grand cosmology

It can be relatively easy to see the field of psychotherapy as consisting of a number of major approaches or perspectives or families such as a psychodynamic perspective, a cognitive behavioral perspective, an existential-humanistic perspective, and so on. It can also be possible to take a larger, perhaps more encompassing view in which the field of psychotherapy is dominated by a more or less single grand cosmology consisting of relatively common foundational beliefs and relatively common answers to the basic questions. Of course there can be variations and modifications, but you can see the field as having a more or less single grand perspective, way of thinking, foundational beliefs, answers to basic questions. You can see a more or less grand cosmology that is the field of psychotherapy.

In other words, most people in the field of psychotherapy probably share a rather similar way of looking at the world, a similar general outlook, whether they say they are following a cognitive school or a behavioral school, an integrative school or a solution-focused school. If all psychotherapists were in a big room, many might agree to the following small sample of what might be called a grand cosmology:

- There is a cumulative body of psychotherapeutic knowledge.
- There are basic needs and drives; in general, most people have similar basic needs and drives.
- Most human beings go through much the same stages of human growth and development.
- The person and the external world interact with and affect one another.
- People generally seek to reduce pain and to enhance pleasure.
- There are mental illnesses, generally referred to as 'mental disorders'.
- Clients seek psychotherapy mainly for relief of their personal problems, their psychological pain and distress, and their mental illness or disorder.
- Psychotherapists have special knowledge which is useful in treating personal problems, psychological pain and distress, and mental illnesses or disorders.
- Psychological problems, pain, distress, mental illnesses or disorders are caused by things that happened earlier in the person's life.
- Treating personal problems, psychological pain and distress, mental illnesses and disorders is helped by (a) talking things over with a psychotherapist; (b) gaining insight and understanding; and (c) gaining a better outlook, perspective, or way of thinking about things.

If you are ready and eager to actively seek a new grand cosmology, you are probably a rare soul in the field of psychotherapy. Yet, if you do have this rare quality, there are some guidelines, some ways you can follow to seek a new grand cosmology.

5.1 Get yourself ready to seek a new grand cosmology
There are some ways, some guidelines, for getting yourself ready, for putting yourself in the right state. Here are seven:

(a) You can be open to a new grand cosmology. You are at least open, receptive, welcoming. You can at least listen. The message you give is along these lines: 'If you believe that you have a new grand cosmology, you can talk to me. I can listen to what you say. I am able to receive and to appreciate what you say. If you are here to tell about a new grand cosmology, I can be a part of your audience.'

(b) You can actively welcome and invite new grand cosmologies. Ask your students to figure out new grand cosmologies. Invite a person with a new grand cosmology to give a talk, offer a seminar, talk to your group. If you are an editor, invite articles offering new grand cosmologies. If you are in charge of conference programs, provide some room for a program on new grand cosmologies.

If there is a list of foundational beliefs, pin a ribbon on approaches, conceptual systems, that decline virtually all of the commonly held foundational beliefs and that instead offer their own, distinctively different foundational beliefs. Search out these new grand cosmologies.

(c) Deliberately put yourself into a state where your relationship to what you hold dear is one in which you can say, with almost whimsical good feeling, 'This notion is really kind of silly, kind of absurd, kind of dumb. Believing in this notion so fervently is kind of silly, absurd, dumb. I truly believe that there are deeper needs and drives? This is a core truth I know is true? Nobody and nothing can get me to give up this idea that I take for granted? Well, clinging to that truth is really kind of ridiculous. I am chuckling. See me chuckling? Grasping such a truth is absurd! Let it go! Let it go straight away!'

Being able to put yourself into this relationship with what you truly hold dear is being able to get creative new ideas by seeking new grand cosmologies.

(d) One of the characteristics of many researchers is a readiness to doubt, to be skeptical. If something is put forward as true, many researchers will set out to test the supposed truth, to check it out. The researcher can ask, 'Is this really true? Does it hold up? I will check it out. I can even see if it is not especially true.'

A researcher's willingness to doubt can proclaim, 'I have doubts about this, so I will check it out.' Suppose that the sense of doubt is encouraged to grow, to become big-time, so that it proclaims, 'In fact, I doubt if any of this is true; the whole idea is wrong; this whole way of looking at things is wrong; there can be a whole new way of looking at all of this; there can be a whole new cosmology!'

There can be a point where the researcher's sense of doubt leads to formulating something to be checked out, and a research hypothesis is born. If you go beyond that point, instead of heading toward a research study, your growing sense of doubt can give rise to a whole new cosmology.

(e) Deliberately put yourself in the role of the one who has big, new, revolutionary ideas. Shift out of the person you ordinarily are and into a qualitatively new state in which you exuberantly and with mean and exciting intention proclaim, 'I have big, new, revolutionary ideas. I look at the field in big, new, revolutionary ways!' If some other part of you or if another person asks, 'So what are your big, new, revolutionary ideas?' you can cheerfully say, 'I have no idea, but I will come up with big, new, revolutionary ideas!'

Putting yourself into the proper state can precede actually having the revolutionary ideas. Indeed, putting yourself into the proper state can set the stage for your actually coming up with the big, new, revolutionary ideas.

(f) You can try to build your own new grand cosmology. Give yourself an opportunity to dip into the creative world of building a whole new cosmology. Once you have a fair picture of the grand cosmology that the field holds dear, see what it is like to try to create a whole new one. Deliberately and intentionally try to build a whole new way of making whole new sense of the entire field of psychotherapy. This is the task that Whitehead (1929; cf. Mays, 1977) set for himself in regard to the fields of mathematics and logic. Accept the challenge of that task for the field of psychotherapy.

Here is a game you can play to come up with a new grand cosmology. Suppose that you are a cognitive-behavioral therapist, and the speaker is a well-known proponent of interpersonal psychotherapy. You may criticize the speaker's approach, show how your approach is better. You can argue with the speaker's approach, find faults and weaknesses in the speaker's approach.

But suppose you go much further. Suppose that you back away from both the speaker's interpersonal psychotherapy and your own cognitive-behavioral psychotherapy. Picture a whole new cosmology that differs from both the interpersonal and the cognitive-behavioral grand ways of seeing things. When you look toward this third cosmology, it is indeed a third option. It is the third grand option that is not the interpersonal or the cognitive-behavioral. What would a cosmology look like if it departed from the interpersonal way of making sense of things, and if it also departed from the cognitive-behavioral way of making sense of things? You are taking steps toward the third grand option. Stay here. Look around. You are in the vicinity of a new grand cosmology. Can you see what it looks like?

(g) Throw yourself into an alien way of looking at things, an alien mind-set, perspective, cosmology. Whatever is your own way of thinking, your own outlook, deliberately undergo a shift into a whole different one. Hurl yourself into a classical psychoanalytic mind-set, a classical cognitive mind-set, a classical experiential mind-set.

Debaters cultivate the skill of moving back and forth between being a proponent of a 'pro'stance and a 'con'stance, being in favor of and against some position on some issue. Actors can cultivate the skill of throwing themselves into being a particular character, of enacting a particular role. In much the same way, move into being an active proponent of a whole different and alien way of looking at things, outlook, perspective, cosmology. If you are a cognitive therapist, hurl yourself into being a classical psychoanalytic practitioner, complete with the psychoanalytic way of making sense of and understanding things.

Find an authoritative chapter proclaiming the classical psychoanalytic position. Grasp the book firmly in both hands, lift up your head, and belt out the statements as if you are the designated spokesman for the classical psychoanalytic position. When you are the fine character actor, you know that you are to be the guilt-ridden mother, sitting with head bowed in the large chair in the living room, hands limp on your lap, being pummeled with the accusatory words of your daughter who is screeching her contempt for the immorality you have committed. When the director says, 'Go!', you can switch from being you to being the character of the mother.

You are practicing so that you are ready to seek a new grand cosmology, but even in practicing the switch usually takes place all at once. The debater who moves from the 'con' position to the 'pro' position makes the switch all at once. The cognitive therapist who is belting out the classical psychoanalytic position makes the switch all at once. The actor who becomes the defined character in the scene does this all at once.

> Just because it is a transition between incommensurables, the transition between competing paradigms cannot be made a step at a time, forced by logic and neutral experience. Like the Gestalt switch, it must occur all at once (though not necessarily in an instant) or not at all! (Kuhn, 1970: 151; cf. Chalmers, 1982)

Practice means becoming able to make this all-at-once switch.

5.2 Be able to recognize a new grand cosmology that is full of creative new ideas

You are to be able to see more than a new grand cosmology that is just different, unique, unlike the ordinary outlooks and ways of looking at things.

Being new and different is good, but it is not necessarily enough. In addition, you are to be able to recognize a cosmology that is full of creative new ideas. Look for and welcome utterly new and different cosmologies that can produce creative new ideas like a popcorn popper produces popcorn. The new cosmology can solve the unsolved problems, can advance the field in leaps and bounds, can open up grand new areas of new knowledge and new discoveries. The new grand cosmology is not only different, it is profusive. It fills the room with creative new ideas.

6. Study the conceptual foundations of approaches with high 'challenge and threat value'

You hold to your own approach. There are other approaches. Getting creative new ideas can come from seeking out and studying the other approaches that have high 'challenge and threat value' to yours. I am not talking about some other approach being more popular than yours, being the fashionably dominant approach. Nor am I talking about an approach that might be your personal rival. In a particular family, two approaches may be rivals, such as humanistic approaches and existential approaches within a larger family to which they both belong.

Instead, I am talking about approaches that have high challenge and threat value to your conceptual foundations, the cornerstones of your approach, your basic principles, your foundational beliefs, the dictums and canons of your approach. Whatever your answers to basic questions, there are approaches whose answers have high challenge and threat value to your answers. Whatever your position on basic issues, there are approaches whose positions bear high challenge and threat value to your position.

There are at least two ways that some other approach has high challenge and threat value.

(a) The other approach is different from yours on almost every cornerstone, every basic principle, dictum and canon, position on basic issues, answer to basic questions. On every foundational belief you can identify, your approach and the alien other approach differ. There can be approaches that share a fair proportion of your conceptual foundations, or a moderate proportion, or a rather low proportion. 'High challenge and threat value' means that the other approach or the other approaches share virtually none of your conceptual foundations. There is virtually nothing in common.

(b) Not only does the other approach have altogether different conceptual foundations, but its conceptual foundations are not at all friendly. They challenge yours, are seriously threatening to yours, are in almost mortal opposition to yours. If you believe in particular kinds of basic needs and drives that are universal, the other approach dispenses with the core idea of needs and drives, and therefore with the further idea that needs and drives are basic and are universal.

You can move into the zone of creative new ideas by carefully examining the conceptual foundations of the approach with such high challenge and threat value. Know the rival conceptual foundations so intimately that you are almost drawn toward adopting them. Study the rival conceptual foundations so well that you are forced to defend yours, to justify clinging to your own.

Deliberately let yourself be open to the creative new ideas that can arise and encompass both your conceptual foundations and theirs, that come when you place your conceptual foundations and theirs in serious opposition, when you seek to account for the fundamental differences between the two sets. Creative new ideas can arise when the two sets of conceptual foundations are studied in opposition to one another.

You believe in certain kinds of basic needs. The enemy conceptual system has no place for the notion of needs or drives. There are no grand pushes or pulls. You begin by being threatened because if the enemy conceptual system wins, then your approach is replaced, is gone, extinguished. Then you try to be democratic. There is room for both your approach and the enemy approach. Then you move on to enlarging your approach to encompass the enemy approach. If you stretch your notion of 'needs' in this particular way, then the enemy approach is no longer a threat. It is assimilated. You have succeeded! You have found a creative new idea, and the creative new idea lets you stay alive and defeat the enemy. Now you have to be quite clear about exactly what the creative idea was. It was here a minute ago. Try to remember exactly what the creative new idea looked like.

It is exceedingly rare for a proponent of one approach to carefully study an approach with high challenge and threat value. It is far more common that proponents of one approach have the thinnest of knowledge of dangerous rivals, perhaps enough to give the impression of knowing it enough to ignore the rival, to catalogue and dismiss it. 'Oh, that's one of those "integrative therapies". Yes, I know about that approach.' But you don't. Creative new ideas come when the proponent of one approach studies the rival approach in serious depth, with one mind eager to understand the guts of the rival approach, and another mind alert to the puffs of creative new ideas that can be stirred by the careful study of the rival approach. Doing this may be rare, but the creative payoff can be exciting.

6.1 You can use rationality to attack what is threatening, or you can follow the trail of the threat to discover the creative new idea

As you study an approach with high challenge and threat value, it is likely that you will come across a sentence or a paragraph or so that leaves you feeling threatened, edgy, defensive, unsettled, attacked, protective of your own way of thinking. You have bodily-felt sensations that are uncomfortable, bothersome, threatening. Now what do you do?

One thing you can do is to use rationality and logic to attack what may be so threatening, to reduce the threat. This is the exceedingly common way of doing something about the threat that comes with an idea of high challenge and threat value. Switch into the mode of rational thought and logical reasoning. The earth is not the center of the universe? The earth revolves around the sun? There are no basic needs and drives? Mental illnesses and disorders are myths? Let us check this out with rationality and logic. Let us point out the inconsistencies in such preposterous notions. Let us take a careful look at the premises, the faulty reasoning. Let us see what research has to say, what is accepted by science, by the cumulative body of knowledge. When you use the weapons of rationality and logic to attack what is threatening, you can usually succeed in successfully attacking what is so threatening. The threat can be reduced, and so are the chances of your finding whatever creative new idea may have been lurking in the near vicinity.

Reasoning and logic can be tools that are precious and have powerful effects. Logic and reasoning can be used for better or for worse. When they are wielded by a skilled artisan, reasoning and logic can be powerfully effective in attacking whatever may be threatening. This is using reasoning and logic 'for worse', because the net effect is to seal off and destroy whatever creative new idea may have been responsible for the threat. Be careful, or you may be successful in your use of reasoning and logic, and you thereby preserve yourself from the creative new idea that led you to use the weapons of reasoning and logic in the first place.

Are reasoning and logic good? One trap is to have as the alternative that reasoning and logic are poor, loose, wrong, or absent. However, reasoning and logic can be seen as not so good when their main uses are (a) to defend against threat, to reduce the threat of some menacing other idea, or (b) to have the net effect of sealing off, closing off, distancing, pushing away a creative new idea. And reasoning and logic are often used, or misused, for these kinds of purposes.

The grand authorities, scholars and scientists rarely proclaim that they reject some idea because the idea is so challenging and threatening. Instead, the grand authorities, scholars and scientists use reasoning and logic in evaluating a new idea. It is so reasonable and logical to use reasoning and logic in evaluating a new idea.

The grand authorities, scholars and scientists did not reject the ideas of Copernicus because they were so challenging and threatening. Not at all. The grand authorities, scholars and scientists judged his ideas by the twin pillars of reasoning and logic to see whether the earth is not really the center of the universe, and to see whether the sun is the center around which the earth revolves. One pillar was to judge whether his ideas fitted in with what was known to be basically true, and the other pillar was to judge whether his ideas fitted in with the cumulative body of scientific knowledge.

What was the reasonable and logical conclusion of this careful evaluation by means of reason and logic? This was the careful conclusion in the words of Clarius:

> Copernicus's position contains many absurd or erroneous assertions: it accepts that the earth is not at the center of the firmament ... that the sun is at the center of the world ... All these things are in conflict with the doctrine commonly received by philosophers and astronomers. Moreover ... these assertions seem to contradict what Holy Scriptures teach us. (Duhem, 1996: 146)

In other words, 'The two censured propositions did not present either of the two characteristics that marked an admissible astronomical hypothesis; therefore, both must be totally rejected' (ibid.). Who could seriously question such fair and honest use of reasoning and logic in judging new ideas?

What is more, the field of psychotherapy uses the same rational reasoning and logic to reject many challenging and threatening ideas today. The field carefully and rationally judges whether the new idea fits in with or violates what the field knows is basically true, and whether the new idea fits in with or violates what is contained in the cumulative body of psychotherapeutic research and knowledge. If the new idea fails the test of reasoning and logic, the new idea is rejected, discarded, declined, marginalized, trivialized and ignored. The field's grand authorities, scholars and scientists' use of reasoning and logic to reject challenging and threatening new ideas would be eminently understandable to the grand authorities, scholars and scientists who rejected the challenging and threatening ideas of Copernicus.

It could be much better if an altogether different brand of reasoning and logic were used to judge challenging and threatening new ideas. The reasoning and logic would be that, if the idea is indeed challenging and threatening, it is reasonable and logical to conclude that the new idea may well be a creative new idea, and reason and logic may then be used to follow the trail of the challenge and the threat to discover the creative new idea that is causing all the fuss.

The common scenario in the field is to be challenged and threatened by the new idea, and then to use reasoning and logic to attack, reject and discard the new idea. A preferred alternative is to acknowledge the challenge and the threat, and to use rationality, reasoning and logic to start from the challenge and the threat to discover the creative new idea that might have been responsible for the challenge and the threat.

Unfortunately, the common scenario is exceedingly common, and the creative alternative is exceedingly rare. Be exceedingly wary of rationality, reasoning and logic used in the service of attacking a new idea. Be appreciative of rationality, reasoning and logic used in the service of discovering the creative new idea behind the challenge and the threat.

6.2 Study the history of failed approaches with high challenge and threat value

Go back 50 years, 100 or 200 years or more. Typically there was a dominant approach and a small number of alternatives, rivals. Then the dominant approach was replaced by another dominant approach and a somewhat revised set of alternatives, rivals.

If you want to find creative new ideas, and you have even a slight flair for the historical, you can do so by looking through history to find the rare and special approaches with sparkling new creative ideas, approaches that fell outside the dominant approaches and their respected alternatives and rivals at the time. Look for approaches with at least the following qualities and characteristics:

(a) They were failures in that they did not catch on. They rarely had any substantive constituency. They were essentially unknown. They failed to reach the status of a contender, a rival to the dominant approach at the time. In this sense, the search can appeal to the dedicated historian because these approaches are hard to locate. Each of these special approaches may have existed as one or two books by a generally unknown author, and the books are typically out of print.

(b) They sharply and severely clashed with the dominant approach at the time. Feyerabend (1972) was one of the leading voices in appreciating the extent to which potentially new and creative ideas can be rejected out of hand simply because they clash with and threaten regnant ways of thinking. Some of these threatening and rejected new ideas can be the seeds of grand approaches that rise up and eventually replace the dominant approaches, the fashionable ways of thinking. This is not the place to look. Instead, the historian searches for those creative new ideas that challenged and threatened the regnant way of thinking but failed to grow into worthy contenders, that shriveled and essentially died. These are the target of your historical search.

(c) They came from and represented a qualitatively new mind-set, way of thinking and seeing things. During the historical era, there usually was a dominant way of thinking and a few rival ways of thinking. Some of the rival ways of thinking were opposite to the dominant way of thinking, so that, if the dominant way of thinking was that the sun revolved around the earth, it is conceivable that a rival way of thinking might be the opposite, i.e. the earth revolved around the sun. They clashed with one another in large part because they were opposites, and yet they all came from a similar kind of mind-set.

Looking for new ideas can mean being on the lookout for some way of thinking that seemed to come from an utterly new mind-set. The sun does not revolve around the earth, nor does the earth revolve around the sun. Instead, be on the lookout for the whole new mind-set that departs from both conceptualizations. It puts the conceptualizations of the time into one basket, and it introduces a whole new basket.

Become a student of history. Look for new ideas by studying the history of failed approaches that seemed to have these three kinds of characteristics. Mach (1960: 316) knew about this way of discovering priceless new ideas:

> We shall recognize also that not only a knowledge of the ideas that have been accepted and cultivated by subsequent teachers is necessary for the historical understanding of a science, but also that the rejected and transient thoughts of the inquirers, nay even apparently erroneous notions, may be very important and instructive ... From the higher point of view at which different paths converge, we may look about us with freer vision and discover routes before unknown.

7. Do 'discovery-oriented research' to enter a world that welcomes creative new ideas

The purpose of most research in the field of psychotherapy is to check out what is believed to be true, to see whether the idea or belief holds up, to test what is hypothesized to be true, to be more confident in what is believed. If the research is done well, the findings can lend some confirmation to what was believed or thought to be true, or the findings can disconfirm, question, challenge what had been thought of as true.

In the field of psychotherapy, the purpose of most research is not to discover new territory. Rather, the purpose is to check out what you believe you see or find in the new territory. The purpose is to do experiments to prove or to disprove, rather than to discover whole new things: 'experimentation is mainly concerned with proof, and rarely leads to discovery' (Bolgar, 1965: 31; cf. Edwards, 1998). Research in the field of psychotherapy is not much of a means of discovering what is new: 'The hallmark role of research is not to innovate, not to discover exciting new therapeutic techniques or interventions' (Kiesler, 1994: 143).

On the other hand, many researchers acknowledge a phase that generally precedes real research, a phase that is looser, less rule-bound, less rigorously systematic. It is a phase of playing around with ideas, of trying out possibilities, of curiosity-driven tinkering, of seeing what can happen if you do this or do that. It is a phase of either thinking of possibilities or of exploring possibilities or of putting them together in a kind of 'thought experiment' (Einstein, 1953). You play around to 'see what follows, without accompanying predictions or explanations ... Exploratory experiment is the probing playful activity by which we get a feel for things. It succeeds when it leads to the discovery of something there' (Schon, 1982: 145). This is not real research, but it leans in the direction of exploration, opening up new territory, coming up with something that can be researched, heading toward new discoveries.

Then, ordinarily, the researcher does real research, almost always to check out what the researcher is to check out, to confirm what the researcher believes to be true, to test the hypothesis. This is the ordinary way research is done. But there is another way, another main purpose and use of research, other than to test hypotheses.

In an alternative mind-set, the purpose and use of research is to discover what is there to be discovered. This means that research shines the light on new territory, exposes the researcher to what has yet to be known, pushes back the outer borders of what is known, explores new ground, uncovers the secrets of psychotherapy, invites the researcher to see what has not been seen and to think about it and know it in ways that are new for the researcher, and removes the curtain from the new world of what can be known, to discover what is there to be discovered. This is the discovery-oriented approach to research on psychotherapy (Mahrer, 1985, 1988, 1996a, 1996b, 2004a; Mahrer and Boulet, 1999).

The discovery-oriented approach takes the researcher by the hand, and leads the researcher into a world that is filled with the fragrance of new ideas, that charms and entices new ideas from the researcher. Step into the discovery-oriented world, and new ideas are swirling all around. Discovery-oriented research shows the researcher more and more of what psychotherapy can achieve, help bring about, accomplish. Discovery-oriented research shows the researcher better and better ways of accomplishing what psychotherapy can accomplish.

Discovery-oriented research lets the researcher see what is new, be face to face with what is new, and that is the elixir for creative new ideas. Discovery-oriented research tells the researcher: 'You see what is new. Now you can have creative new ideas about all of this. Here is something extraordinary, unusual, wonderful, alien, surprising, unknown, inexplicable. Now you can wallow in creative new ideas. You can see psychotherapy in a whole new way. Let yourself have the creative new ideas that are starting to flutter.' Learn what discovery-oriented research is, then participate in it or at least get close to this kind of research. Enter a world of discovery-oriented research that welcomes creative new ideas.

How can you come up with creative new ideas? This chapter suggests that one answer is to find and use ways to adopt a creative new perspective on the field of psychotherapy, or at least on the subject matter you are studying. But that is a big job. In case you ask, 'All right, so how do I go about adopting some sort of creative new perspective?', this chapter has suggested seven guidelines, principles, ways to do this.

I hope that you find one or more of the suggested ways to be interesting and appealing and sensible enough for you to try them out, for you to become proficient in using them, and especially for you to put them to work helping you to come up with creative new ideas.

I also hope that you can improve this method of finding and adopting a creative new perspective on the field or on your particular part of the field. This method works. It will be up to you to keep making it better.

CHAPTER 4

Use 'Bodily-felt Sensations' as Tracking Guides to Creative New Ideas

The idea is rather simple. You begin by putting yourself into a state of readiness to look for creative new ideas. Picture yourself as saying out loud, or as almost being the inner voice saying, 'I am going to search for creative new ideas; I am ready to find a creative new idea.' You have no idea what that creative idea may be. You are merely ready to search. You may be using one of the other methods described in this volume, or you may be emphasizing the way of using your 'bodily-felt sensations' as tracking guides.

Once you program yourself to the search for creative new ideas, once you begin the journey, you can depend upon and use your immediately fluctuating bodily-felt sensations as sensitive tracking guides. They essentially can let you know that you are getting warmer or colder, closer to or further from the creative new idea.

1. There is a flow of bodily-felt sensations occurring inside you

If you turn your attention to what is happening in your body, you can usually be aware of a world of bodily-felt sensations. These can include a coldness in your feet, a tingling in your hands, a gentle light touch of the blood beating in or near your eyes, a heaviness in the belly, a thickening of the tongue, light electrical tinglings across the chest, slight dizziness inside the head, a juiciness in the genitals, tightening of the nipples, quivering in the hands, shivers down the spine, tightening of the muscles in the abdomen, quickening of the heartbeat, thickening of the lips, warmth in the lower back, itchiness in the scalp, hollowness in the chest region.

When you are on a search for a creative new idea, these bodily-felt sensations can fall into at least two groups, and each group can serve as a flashing light, a signal, that you are heading in the right direction. One group comprises bodily-felt sensations of excitement, titillation, arousal, thrill. Your body feels lighter and on happy edge. Your breath is faster and shallower. You are excited, and that means you are closer to the creative new idea. Another group, another light or signal, comprises bodily-felt sensations of ominous threat, something is wrong, something is out of order. Be careful. Watch out. Be on guard. There is a clutching up in your stomach. Your eyes and ears are on alert. There is a breathless quiet. Both the sense of excited happiness and the sense of ominous threat are signals that you are coming closer to the creative new idea.

2. Use the bodily-felt signals to tell you that you are close to a creative new idea

Most people, most of the time, are not aware of this flow of bodily-felt sensations until they somehow become pronounced, conspicuous. Then you can be aware of a pounding headache or a cramping of the calf muscles or a tightness in the lower back. Many of these bodily-felt sensations are more internal and are more subtle, such as a sense of lightness in the head, a sense of something falling into place, an awareness of a rising up of something in the chest region, or a concentration of the muscles around the eyes.

When you are trying hard to think, to figure out something, to arrive at an answer, it is easy to pay little or no attention to these bodily-felt sensations. Your attention is on what you are thinking about. However, you can also be attuned to those special moments where you are thinking hard, and you have bodily-felt sensations of arousal, excitement, or bodily-felt sensations of threat, ominousness, something is wrong. Either of these bodily-felt signals can tell you that the creative new idea is right here, so very close.

This is the point at which the bodily-felt sensations are trying to get your attention: 'See the flashing lights? Hear the buzzer?' The bodily-felt sensations are jumping up and down, trying to get you to see that you are in the close vicinity of a creative new idea. You may be having the bodily-felt sensations of excitement and arousal at being so close. Or you may be having bodily-felt sensations of an ominous threat, the scary risk of being in the close vicinity of a creative new idea. In either case, stop. Look around. You can be touching or touched by the creative new idea.

3. Here are some guidelines for using the bodily-felt sensations

There can be different times and places, and different ways, to use these bodily-felt sensations as tracking guides to new ideas.

3.1 Use both careful reasoning and bodily-felt sensations

When you are trying to solve some problem, to figure something out, you can rely on careful reasoning. Follow the track of careful reasoning. If you find yourself off the track, stop and use careful reasoning to get you back on track. Keep using careful reasoning to move you forward.

However, you can combine careful reasoning and bodily-felt sensations. As you are thinking carefully, figuring it out, you can also be aware that right here the light goes on. Right here are bodily-felt sensations of arousal and excitement or of threat and scary vigilance. Reasoning stops for a moment, and the bodily-felt sensations indicate that you are in the very close vicinity of a creative new idea. Reasoning brought you into breathing distance of a creative new idea. Bodily-felt sensations tell you that the creative new idea is right here.

3.2 Enter into the creative world of absurd possibilities

When you are thinking and ruminating, you can leave the world of ordinary reality and enter into the creative world of absurd possibilities. Leave the ordinary world that is rooted in reality. Enter into the world of wholesale unreality, free of reality constraints, not limited or rooted in what is real and true. Let go of the world of what is known, of what is real and true, of what is accepted, taken for granted. Enter the world of absurd possibilities.

Enter the creative world of the bizarre, the ridiculous, the utterly fictitious. Enter into the world that is ordinarily known as the world of madness, of having lost one's mind, of being demented, mindless, crazy, psychotic, the world of lunacy.

Enter into the creative world of absurd possibilities. William James provides one of the classic descriptions of this special world that 'functions according to laws unknown to waking consciousness, provides information in no clear way connected with the senses, and transcends the limitations of time and space as defined by rational consciousness' (Taylor, 1984: 43).

Suppose that you start with some issue, some problem, some possibility.

You are ruminating about where it all started in the first place, how a person gets to be the way the person is. There can be three sets of bodily-felt sensations that indicate you are leaving the ordinary realm, entering into and then being in the creative world of absurd possibilities: (a) When you are detaching from, letting go of, the ordinary world of ordinary rationality, of reality constraints, you may have bodily-felt sensations of unease, disquiet, some fear, anticipatory rumbling of something ominous to come, a rupturing of what is the familiar, the known. (b) When you are beginning to enter into the creative world of absurd possibilities, there can be bodily-felt sensations of lightness, giddiness, dizziness, floating, titillation, tingling, silliness, giggling. (c) When you have entered into this world, are living and being in this creative world of absurd possibilities, these absurd possibilities can be the new reality, can be the door to seeing so much more, and the bodily-felt sensations can be those of enlightenment, liberation, freedom, clarity, a new knowingness, other-worldliness, peacefulness, serenity.

3.3 When you are drifting in thoughts, bodily-felt sensations can let you know when you arrive at a creative new idea

Start by concentrating on some issue, some problem, some question. Start with questions such as these: where does it all come from in the first place? how come that person's qualitative shift lasted long after the session ended? what is the fatal flaw in doing research for that reason? Once you pick out an issue or problem or question, burn it into your mind. Wallow in it. Soak yourself in it. Put it at the center of all your attention.

Then cast adrift in the free flow of thoughts, ideas, mental pictures, mental images. Let go of the initial issue or problem or question, and drift around in thoughts and pictures, ideas and images. Let them come and go. Just observe them with as little involvement as possible. Be drugged. Do not think about the free flow of pictures and images. Do not guide them or label them or recognize them or have thoughts about them. Just let them be. Let them come and go.

But always be receptive to the clanging of the bodily-felt sensations that say, 'You have arrived at a creative new idea! It is here, somewhere very close!' Those bodily-felt sensations will go off suddenly. They are exciting or scary, but they suddenly go off. You have to be receptive and open to hearing them. It is as if they go off and wake you out of your free-floating reverie of thoughts and images.

And then you stop. Look around. See where you are when you stop. See where you have arrived. It is likely that you have arrived at a creative new idea. It is right here. It may be related to the initial problem or issue or question that you started with. Or it may be an unrelated but creative new idea.

3.4 When you are enveloped by a cloud of ambiguity, bodily-felt sensations can indicate that a creative new idea is hidden inside the cloud of ambiguity

This begins when you are in a relatively clear state as you are thinking, reading, talking, listening. You are relatively clear about what you are thinking, reading, talking about, listening to. Then something happens. Things become vague, cloudy, ambiguous, hazy, unclear. You are aware that you are enveloped by a cloud of ambiguity.

You are aware of this shift when you are no longer especially clear about what you are reading or hearing. The meaning has receded. You are no longer following. Things are somewhat hazy. It is as if your attention is no longer on the topic, the issue. Instead, you have either entered into or been taken over by a cloud of hazy ambiguity. You are numb, drugged, unknowing. You may have been in this cloudy state for a fraction of a second or perhaps 5–15 seconds or more.

Sometimes this momentary state is relatively free of feelings. However, there are special times when you are aware of feelings such as a sense of excitement, being aroused, a sense of watchful vigilance, guardedness. There may even be a sense of peripheral ominousness, disturbance, threat. Something is happening. Something is going on. You have these feelings. You are aware of these feelings. They can be the indications that there is a creative idea somewhere close, perhaps inside or underneath the cloud of ambiguity.

This is where you stop. Hold everything. You are going to start looking around, probing, exploring. There is a creative idea here somewhere. Your job is to find what it is. Right now, you do not know what it is, but you are fairly keen that it is here somewhere. Let the cloud of ambiguity become clearer. Probe beneath the cloud. Perhaps the cloud arose when you approached too close to the creative new idea. Stay here. Search for the creative new idea.

3.5 Use the threatening bodily-felt sensations that precede the 'rush to rejection'

When you are in the vicinity of a creative new idea, when you are confronted by a creative new idea, you may be thoroughly unaware of recognizing what is there in front of you, or nearby or almost breathing on you. Instead, you can be aware of bodily-felt sensations that are threatening. You are bothered, disturbed, on edge. Something is wrong. You can be aware of a tightening up against something, a heightening of wary vigilance, a sense of ominousness, a quickening of the blood, a heightening of pressure. Your bodily-felt sensations prepare you to run away, to erect barriers, to dislike and even hate an enemy.

When you are reading, you begin to feel tight, critical, distracted. You lose interest. You want to put the book down, turn to something else. When you are listening to the other person, you become uncomfortable, your body feels heavy, your eyes narrow, your attention wanders from what he is saying, you notice things about him that you don't like. You are undergoing bothersome and threatening bodily-felt sensations.

When you are gripped by these bodily-felt sensations, it is so easy to automatically give in to the 'rush to rejection'. These bodily-felt sensations so easily propel you into a state of rushing to reject whatever brought forth the bothersome bodily-felt sensations. You are propelled to find good reasons to reject the bothersome, disturbing idea. There is little or no research support. There is an authoritative body of knowledge that refutes the idea. The idea violates what the field knows is true. The idea is bad, wrong, inadequate, fragmented, loose. The idea must be rejected, and here are the careful, organized, rational, systematic, authoritative reasons why the idea is to be rejected.

The 'rush to reject' justifies attacking the proponents of the bad idea and the arguments and evidence put forth by the proponents. What they say is redundant, poorly organized, lacks proper reasons and rationale, is vague and hazy, is poorly referenced. What they say is offensive, overly critical, disrespectful, antagonistic, unprofessional, nasty, provocative, bad. They are proposing the idea because they want to criticize what the field takes for granted, because they like challenging and provoking, because they lack a thorough understanding of the relevant research, because they are wrong-headed, think poorly, don't know any better.

Instead of giving in to the rush to rejection, stay with the bodily-felt sensations. Resist the temptation to find sensible and reasonable reasons to reject the threatening new idea that you probably cannot even put into words. Instead, use the bodily-felt sensations. What makes me so threatened? What makes my body tighten up, get ready for battle, want to reject whatever is doing this to me?

When you are beginning to have negative reactions, to dislike and to object to what you are reading or hearing, it is as if you are at a choice point. (a) You can assemble good and proper reasons for rejecting what you are reading or hearing. Find its faults, its shortcomings. Identify its inconsistencies. Find the serious problems in its logic and reasoning, its knowledge of the relevant literature, its tone and style. Or (b) you can set out to find what it could be that arouses such negative reactions, that is so threatening, off-putting, scary, provocative, challenging.

Look around for the creative new idea that is having all these effects. Try to identify the culprit. What could be doing all this to you? Set aside the negative bodily-felt sensations. Avoid giving in to the rush to rejection. Look around, and find the source of these bodily-felt sensations. You can identify a creative new idea.

3.6 Spell out the creative new idea, using bodily-felt sensations as a guide in finding the precisely right words

You will come in the near vicinity of what seems to be a creative new idea. You are excited because you are sure the creative new idea is right here. You are sure that you can talk about it, tell about it, say what it is. You can carry the creative new idea around with you. You have it in your hands.

But it is not yet precise. You haven't written it down exactly. It is still a little vague, not precisely formed. It is still rough around the edges, somewhat out of focus. Your job is to write it down carefully and precisely. In a sentence or so, say what the creative new idea is, and be precise, accurate, clear. Find and use the precisely right words. This is the final piece of work in coming up with a creative new idea. It is not writing about a creative new idea. It is spelling it out exactly and precisely.

Use the bodily-felt sensations as guides. They can say that this is not quite the right word, you are close but keep searching. Breathing can be shallow. You are almost there. And the guide can tell you that you have found the right word. You have the precise right words. These words fit. The creative new idea is now here, in these exact words. Congratulations. It is time to celebrate.

This chapter can be a friendly invitation, because, even when you are just starting out, a reasonable use of your bodily-felt sensations can bring you face to face with a creative new idea. When you get a little better, even at a journeyman level of competence, then this method seems to have three parts:

(a) Start by putting yourself on a track toward finding or coming up with a creative new idea. Set out on the journey. This is more than merely proclaiming that you would like to find some wonderful new idea. It is more than merely wanting. Instead, the start consists of setting out to explore, to figure out, to solve, to search here and there. You are trying to find the creative new idea.

(b) Use your own bodily-felt sensations as tracking guides. Trust them. Follow them over here, down there, over that other way. Use them to guide you back away. This is not the right direction. You are getting colder. You are heading in the right direction. You are close by.

(c) When the bodily-felt sensations have done their job and you have dutifully followed them, you can be within touching or breathing distance of a creative new idea. It is now up to you to properly identify the creative new idea. Spell it out. Be specific, bring it to explicit and concrete life as an identifiable real thing.

CHAPTER 5

Study the Problem to Come up with Creative New Ideas

You may decide that the problem you want to work on, to solve, is that the window is stuck, or that the roof leaks, or the woman spends her day trying to flush towels down the toilets, or you want to know the best treatment for an abusive personality, or you are seeking to trace the origins of personality back to the initial beginning in the life of the person.

It can be relatively easy to identify the problem, to define something as a problem, to label it in such a way that it is indeed a problem, and then to shift attention over to what to do about the problem, how to fix it, to reduce it, to try to get rid of the problem.

When you follow this common route, (a) you have already selected out that particular phenomenon to deal with, study, work on; (b) you have already labeled it in some way, named it as a given 'problem'; and (c) you have shifted most of your attention to something else about the problem, for example, what may have caused it, how severe it is, what to do about it. By following this common route, you have already sailed by at least two grand opportunities to study the problem so as to be able to come up with creative new ideas. One was when you labeled the problem in some way, rather than studying it further, without some identifying label or name. A second missed opportunity was when you shifted most of your attention away from the problem in, for example, looking for its cause or how to do something about it.

Here are a number of ways to use these opportunities to put attention on the problem so as to capitalize on the possibility of coming up with some creative new ideas:

1. Creative new ideas can come as you are trying to clarify the precise nature of the problem

Picture many practitioners or researchers looking at something they think of as perhaps a problem, and intent on seeing just what it is. 'Is it a problem? What is this problem like? Let me know a little more about this thing that may be a problem.' Now picture the practitioner or researcher nodding, and saying, 'I see. I know what this problem is. I do believe I have clarified the nature of the problem. It is a communication problem …' Or it is called a sexual dysfunction problem, an abusive personality problem, a gender identity problem, a depression problem, a problem of anomie, of ego diffusion, an attention deficit hyperactivity problem.

When the above practitioner or researcher has clarified the nature of the problem, picture another practitioner or researcher who is still puzzling over it, who looks at it this way and that way, who pokes it a little here and there, who looks carefully at this part and that part. Now picture the practitioner or researcher looking and looking, thinking and thinking and then blinking, looking up and away from the problem and saying, 'I think I just got nudged by a creative new idea!'

Here are some ways to come up with creative new ideas as you are trying to clarify the precise nature of the problem:

1.1 Beware of problems that are vague, loose, cloudy, airy-fairy; prefer problems that can provide concretely specific, real pictures

Creative new ideas seem to come more easily if you decline problems that are vague, loose, cloudy, airy-fairy, and if you instead put your attention on problems that lend themselves to pictures that are concretely specific, real. The hard part is backing away from problems that are vague, loose, cloudy, yet seem so compelling. It can be hard to accept that creative ideas are unlikely to occur as you are puzzling about vague and cloudy problems that are common, appealing, and fun to talk about. Giving up and backing away from such problems can be very hard to do. It can be hard to apply the test that if you cannot see the problem in the form of concretely specific, real pictures, you may as well let go of trying to solve the problem.

You can have creative new ideas if you deal with concretely real problems of concretely real phenomena. You can come up with such creative new ideas as momentum, energy and mass if you work on concretely real phenomena:

> Concepts like momentum, energy, and mass were not simply 'there' in
> nature. They emerge by dint of great human effort (in this instance, the

effort of such figures as Descartes, Huygens, and Newton) in response to problems of characterizing real phenomena. (Simon, 1996: 169)

You can have creative new ideas that are abstract when the problem is concretely real, but it is unlikely that you will have creative new ideas if you are facing problems that are loose, cloudy, vague and airy-fairy.

You may or you may not have concretely specific pictures if you put your attention on vague and loose problems such as these: (a) How can the field of psychotherapy progress by integrating the concept of assimilative broadening? (b) What are the parameters of core conceptual schemata? (c) What are the relations between ego diffusion and sensate inhibitor potentials? If you can see these problems in terms of concretely specific pictures, the likelihood of coming up with creative new ideas is higher than if you cannot. If you cannot, then are you able to seriously consider the likelihood of abandoning these particular problems, if only because the chances of coming up with creative new ideas are rather low?

1.2 Creative new ideas can come when you put virtually all your attention on the problem

To begin with, it is helpful if the problem is in a relatively clear form, is in a concretely specific form, is pictured in some detail, rather than being cloudy and loose and vague.

Ordinarily, you put a fair amount of attention on the problem. You are thinking about the problem, but you can be somewhat aware that you are thinking about the problem. Suppose that you go much further so that virtually all your attention is locked onto the problem. So much of your attention is poured into seeing and being concerned with the problem that you are no longer aware that you are thinking hard about the problem. This is the key. It is relatively rare that you actually pour virtually all your attention onto a problem. This is a skill that one must have.

Ordinarily, when you are thinking about some problem, you can still be aware of thoughts such as, 'I think I am getting close', 'This is hard to solve', 'This problem is like that other problem. I should be able to solve this problem.' These kinds of thoughts indicate that there can be substantially more attention targeted on the problem, instead of being available for having such thoughts

Even for people who are dedicated problem-analyzers and problem-solvers, it can be a rare and special experience to put almost all one's attention on the problem so that there is essentially no awareness of time, of where one is, of the nature of the original target problem. The person is truly fixated on the problem, fully lost in thoughts, wholly attentive to the problem.

This is when new ideas can appear. This is when creative new ideas can come about. They appear off to the side, in the periphery, beyond the penumbra. They come and go in a flash. They can seem disconnected from the problem, like new or different ideas, like free associations, like unrelated ideas. You are in a state of receiving creative new ideas, usually without being able to recognize them as new ideas because so much of your attention is poured onto the problem. Suddenly, what appears in front of you is something that you do not recognize immediately as the answer, the solution, but there it is. Instead of the hub and spokes of a wheel, which you had been pursuing, what suddenly appears is a spiral staircase. All of a sudden you are seeing something that proves to be the critical commonality you were searching for. As you are staring fixedly at the problem, it is replaced and you are seeing a simple formula. You are concentrating on how A could lead to B, and there in front of you is the image of B leading to A. The answer comes to you, it simply appears, brought forward by dedicated and concentrated attention.

It can be easier to identify the creative new ideas as creative new ideas when you 'wake up', when you come out of a state of having virtually all of your attention on the problem. You are able to think, 'That is a solution! I do believe that can solve the problem!'

1.3 Even when you are doing other things, let a part of you keep working on the problem

You are attending to the problem as you are trying to get the problem more and more clear, and as you are trying to solve the problem. It is early in the morning and you are sitting in your study. You then turn off the computer, put away the pen and paper, and are ready to go about the day. Creative ideas can come when you can allow a part of you to keep working on the problem. It is as if this small part of you keeps trying to clarify and to resolve the problem even as you go about your day. This little part, in your mind, off to the side, is quietly whispering, 'Now here is as far as I got in making this problem clear, and in looking for a solution. I am going to keep working, but I am going to keep an eye out for solutions coming from whatever is happening outside.' That part keeps working on the problem and is ready to find helpful cues in whatever the person is doing as the person goes through the day. The question the part asks is along these lines: 'How can what I am doing right now, what is happening right now, help me further clarify and maybe solve the problem I am working on?'

For example, you are puzzling about getting clearer on, and maybe solving, the problem of how to enable patients to attain a level of relatively strong feeling quickly, in a session, and to remain at that state throughout the session. This issue is somewhere in your mind as you are brushing your teeth, as the two of you make breakfast and chat, as you put your key in the ignition, park the car in that spot, look for the notes for the committee meeting, walk to the dentist's office, lie back in the dental chair, open your mouth wide. That's it! You are suddenly clear on the problem and a solution! It happened when the dentist said, 'Lean back and assume the position. Mouth open wide …'

The issue is suddenly clear. The solution is suddenly clear. Simply explain to your patients that they are to go to a state of relatively strong feeling and stay there for the session. Tell them! Just give simple instructions and whatever explanation helps. That is the answer, it seems. People do not ordinarily lean back and open their mouths wide, and stay like that. Not in restaurants or in banks or while driving cars or talking to friends. Such a position would be unnatural, out of place. But in a dental chair, it is natural, fitting, and the dentist simply says to do it. What a simple solution, and it came from keeping the matter in the back of your mind as you went through your day. This is a way to allow for creative new ideas.

Suppose that you have been puzzling for months about the matter of the origins of personality, how and where the origins occurred, perhaps when the person was an infant. You have been getting ideas, but the question is still there on your mind. Suppose that one of your favorite times to wonder about answers to that question is when you are in bed, ready to fall asleep.

This particular time, you wake up with a dream. You record the dream because dreams are important to you, and you typically record the dream and then, if it is during the middle of the night, you go back to sleep. As you are getting ready to fall asleep, your mind is going over the dream you have just recorded, and it is as if another part of your mind is also stewing over the long-standing question of where personality comes from in the first place.

This is when the creative idea comes. Here is the answer! The characters in the dream scene are the characters in your infancy! In the dream, you are yelling at the woman you are living with because she brought your ex-wife into your home, and she did so without informing you beforehand. How would this suggest an answer to your long-standing question? Perhaps the person you are in the dream is your father, during your infancy. The person you are yelling at is your mother, during your infancy. And the disliked and unwanted ex-wife is you, in your infancy. Your origins include scenes in which your father yelled at your mother for having you in the first place, and you are the unwanted, disliked infant that your father did not want and disliked because your mother had you without letting him know beforehand!

The creative new idea comes from keeping the question in your mind even as you are doing other things such as thinking about your recorded dream. The creative new idea has a bonus of allowing another way to use dreams, and a bonus of new light on your sense of 'I-ness'.

1.4 *Instead of taking for granted how something took place, clarify the details of how it could have happened*

Clarifying the problem, getting reasonably clear on what the problem is, can often run into pockets of vagueness where you are invited to accept the vagueness, leave things ambiguous, certainly not delve into details. However, if you keep delving into the details of how this could have happened, if you go into the pockets of vague ambiguity, then you can enter the domain of creative new ideas. The creative new ideas rise out of the little details of clarifying how it could have happened.

Some novelists know this trick. Some detectives know this trick. Some scientists know this trick. Don't be fooled with the vague pocket of ambiguity about how something occurred. Everyone is taking for granted that the door was locked from the inside, but if we go through the details of how the door was locked, then it becomes clear that the door could not have been locked from the inside. Here comes the creative idea, born of the beautiful details of just how the event could have occurred.

She was presenting her case at the conference, and opened by saying that she spent the first half-hour or so getting this and that information, on the basis of which she decided to adopt the 'attachment theory' conceptual system, which she proceeded to summarize for the audience before launching into her description of what happened over the next 25 sessions. When she explained that she decided to adopt the attachment theory conceptual system on the basis of the information she had gathered, most of the audience seemed to understand, some nodded.

One young member of the audience was puzzled. He was trying to clarify how she arrived at the attachment theory conceptual system to begin with. He had trouble clarifying how that could be done. However, by now she was well into her description of the case, so he waited until what seemed to be an appropriate time during the question period. Then he asked how he might replicate what she did, how he could get information, for a half-hour or more, on the basis of which he could then decide to use, of the various approaches, the attachment theory approach. He wanted to know what information she got, how that information led her to adopt the attachment theory approach, and especially what conceptual system she used to get the information, particularly the information she looked for and got.

She said that she used no system or approach at all in getting the 30 minutes of information. Yet, when she told some of the information she had gathered, it seemed that this information was mainly from an attachment theory conceptual system rather than from a social learning theory approach or an Adlerian theory approach, or several other approaches. However, maybe he was wrong. This young fellow was almost directly facing an intriguing matter: can information be gathered without being guided by some conceptual system? How can a person gather information and then select a conceptual system that is not the conceptual system from which the initial information was gathered? This young fellow was in the vicinity of some creative new ideas, and he arrived in the vicinity mainly by following what the presenter said carefully enough not to merely take for granted what seemed vague and ambiguous, and instead to try to clarify the details of how the presenter could have arrived at this particular conceptual approach.

Consider another case conference in which a psychiatrist was describing his patient as psychotic. The patient had delusions and hallucinations. Perhaps the most serious, the psychiatrist explained, was seeing his deceased grandmother occasionally in the evening. Although she died six years ago, he saw her at the end of his bed. The grandmother asked him about his day and stayed until he was ready to fall asleep. At this point, a young counseling student was puzzled. She raised her hand. 'Excuse me, doctor, but I am not clear. You said that he had been close to his grandmother, and that she had died about six years ago. Is that right?' The doctor nodded and explained to the young student: 'Yes, you got it right. And one of the symptoms of his psychosis is his seeing her at night. Do you know the difference between a delusion and a hallucination?' The young student laughed, 'I don't think I do, but where I am not clear is how you knew that he was close to his grandmother and that she had died about six years ago.' The psychiatrist carefully explained, 'He told me in the intake interview,' and then turned away to proceed with his case description.

The young counseling student raised her hand again, and the psychiatrist acknowledged the interference in a politely tolerant manner. The student was still puzzled: 'I am still mixed up. Please pardon me, but it seems that you accept that what the patient says is realistic when he tells you that he is close to his grandmother and that she died about six years ago and that he talks with her before he goes to sleep, and then, if those things are real and true, he must be psychotic. Right? But if he is psychotic, then how come you accept as real or true the things he says, on the basis of which you say that we should not accept as real and true the things he says? If he is psychotic, shouldn't we think that his saying he was close to her, and that she died six years ago, and that she talks with him at night are all not real and true? I know I am talking too much, and I get confused easily, but can you clear this up for me?'

Right after the psychiatrist blurted out: 'That would take too much time!', the case conference was replaced by a serious discussion of the standard practice of diagnosing psychosis on the basis of evidence as real and true, which would seem to disenfranchise that evidence as real and true. Creative new ideas may well come from clarifying the details of how something could have happened, rather than meekly and unquestioningly accepting how it happened.

A third example occurred at a workshop in which the presenter was showing how to get inside the patient's world and see the world from the patient's perspective. The presenter explained how the patient was severely depressed. 'Notice how much you can understand the patient by seeing the patient's world from the patient's own perspective.' A young student was puzzled and asked the presenter to explain how the student could do this. 'Excuse me, but I have two problems here. Please can you help me? One is that I believe that if I see the world through the patient's perspective I will be just as depressed as the patient. Is that right or am I wrong? The other thing I am mixed up about is, if I am really being in the patient's perspective, won't I just stay being in the patient's perspective? I mean, how do I get out of being in the patient's perspective? Or am I just being in the patient's perspective a little bit?'

The presenter grinned. 'Can anyone answer his questions? I don't think I can answer those questions!' In the coffee break, the presenter and the student talked much more about the student's confusion, and the presenter encouraged the young student to keep puzzling about those questions.

The teacher was telling the psychotherapy class how important it is for the therapist to be open, honest, authentic and congruent in relating to the client. Later, the teacher was showing the class how to use clinical inferences in, for example, figuring out how to formulate an interpretation or an empathic response, how to assess and evaluate diagnostic cues that the therapist observes, and how to draw inferences from the way the client is being in relationship with the therapist. The class was busy taking notes. Except for one student.

It was at this point that the student expressed her confusion: 'How do I go about being open, honest, authentic and congruent, and also having a private stream of clinical inferences? Do I alternate between the two, or do I try to do both at the same time? Do I openly and authentically tell the client that I am figuring out how to formulate my interpretation, or that I am evaluating a diagnostic cue that I just observed? I am trying to see how I can do both.'

At this point the teacher had a private inference about whether this student belonged in the program, given her 'attitude problem'. The student was genuinely perplexed, and did not get much of an answer to her question.

Perhaps this student had the makings of someone who could have creative new ideas because, unlike the others, instead of merely taking for granted how something took place, she was able to clarify the details of how something actually could have taken place. One of the conditions for creative new ideas is a readiness and ability to spell out the details of how something could have occurred. Walk through the details.

Creative new ideas can come (a) when your careful walking through of the details brings you face to face with a compelling puzzle: 'It seems that what we took for granted as having happened just could not have happened.' Creative new ideas can come (b) when your careful walking through of the details leans hard toward showing that it almost certainly happened this way, rather than the way we all took for granted. Creative new ideas can come (c) when your careful walking through of the details shows that it almost certainly happened this way, even though no one had considered it happening this way.

1.5 Pay special attention to the surprisingly inexplicable
Every so often, something inexplicable can happen in the session. It is surprising, hard to understand, but here it is. Pay attention to these occurrences because they can be rich in creative possibilities.

These surprisingly inexplicable occurrences can happen in at least three ways. One way is that they just seem to occur. As far as you are concerned, you do nothing to help bring it about. Indeed, it can be hard to tell what accounts for this inexplicable event, but here it is. All of a sudden, the person you are working with seems to be the little girl you played with before you started going to school. She lived in the next apartment and, for a few moments, this person is surely that little girl. Or, while you are listening to the patient talk, you are surprisingly aware of a voice coming from just behind your head, whispering, 'I can show you a card trick,' and what the voice says has nothing to do with what is happening in the session. Or the whole office suddenly seems to be revolving counterclockwise, and this lasts for four to six seconds and then goes away. Or you are concentrating on what he is saying, and he suddenly seems to become a whole new person, altogether different, for a lengthy few seconds or so.

A second way is when you suddenly do something that is truly inexplicable. You do it all of a sudden, out of the blue. It is quite out of character for you. It is not something you have thought about, even briefly considered. It is not something brilliant, a clever and bold therapeutic stroke. Nor is it something you should not do, something unethical, harmful, hurtful. It is just something inexplicable, challengingly hard to fathom.

In the course of the session, you are startled to hear your immediate stream of private thoughts being spoken out loud, by you! It is as if your inner thoughts are coming through your mouth. 'She's accepting my interpretation. Good.' 'He's searching my face for cues about how I'm reacting to his disclosure.' How could this be? It is your own voice saying these private thoughts.

You suddenly find yourself in a short burst of giddiness and silliness, and you are taken over by almost uncontrollable laughter. It lasts for almost 15 seconds. You are just as startled as the patient. You had no hints of this coming. What either of you said was not especially funny, nor was it especially serious and sober. Your laughter was not ridiculing the patient nor coming from something that just came to mind. It was certainly alien, out of keeping with your professional character, and wholly inexplicable.

For a brief second you wonder whose voice it is, then you realize that the voice is coming from you, though it is not your ordinary voice speaking to the patient: 'Your middle name is ancient … You like walking in light rain … You used to be left-handed…' You have not been drifting in thoughts or seeing images floating by. You have not been having such thoughts. You aren't even thinking whether the words have anything to do with what the two of you were talking about. You are mainly just surprised by the unrecognized voice and the content of the words. All of this is inexplicable.

A third way is when what you ordinarily do seems to result in a consequence that is both extraordinary and inexplicable. You can understand and expect that what you ordinarily do will not produce the ordinary and expected consequence each time, or even most of the time. Sometimes it just doesn't work. But this is different. The apparent consequence is both unusual and challengingly inexplicable.

Your common responses include mild and simple reflections of feeling. Sometimes patients indicate some acceptance. Sometimes patients simply continue talking. This has happened with this patient too, except that in this particular instance the patient seemed so happily startled that you momentarily wondered what you had said. She grinned, sat bolt upright, and giggled delightfully. You have no idea whatsoever what has just happened. It is inexplicable.

One of the things you often do is to provide mild and rather gentle interpretations. Sometimes you merely raise a little doubt about what the patient has just taken for granted, or you speculate whether there might be another way of thinking about what the patient is describing. You rarely push or even slightly insist or seem to differ much with what the person is saying. He is saying that he is not especially looking forward to going to his parents' place because dad will be the way he usually is. That is all the patient says, with mild feeling, and all you say, as a soft aside, with equally little feeling, is : 'Well, maybe ...' That's all you say, yet he seems as if a bolt of happy lightning has struck him, his eyes open wide, he seem electrified: 'YES! That's it! It can be SO different! I never thought about that before! THIS IS SO GREAT!' Even playing the tape over and over again, you have not even the slightest idea what happened. It is genuinely inexplicable.

Here you are, face to face with something that is surprisingly inexplicable. It is challenging you to do something. You can simply label it as something surprisingly inexplicable, a genuine exception, and let it go at that. In other words, you can essentially do nothing and proceed to something else. Or you can drain it of its exceptional quality by giving it an easy and cheap explanation. In other words, you can essentially explain it away and proceed to something else.

If the surprisingly inexplicable phenomenon could talk, it might plead with you: 'I am surprisingly inexplicable, so please study me carefully. Respect me as surprisingly inexplicable. I can contain the seeds of creative new ideas, so try to study me to uncover these creative possibilities.' Go ahead. Accept the challenge, the opportunity.

1.6   A second wave of creative ideas can come by carefully clarifying the initial creative idea

Creative new ideas usually start with some problem that you are working on. Trying to clarify the problem can give rise to an initial creative idea. In any case, here you are with a creative idea inside your head. Or at least it seems to be a creative new idea. It seems to bear the hallmarks of a creative new idea.

But there is a danger. The idea is still there, somewhere in your head. It is somewhat vague. It is unspecified, not quite clear. The danger is that, if you try to clarify exactly what it is, the idea can vanish. Poof, it is gone. The more you try to see it head on, directly, the more it vanishes. It is tempting to leave the creative new idea vague. Don't even try to clarify it or it will be gone. That is the danger.

The important suggestion is to work hard at clarifying that creative idea. Write it down in actual words. Find the precise words to formulate the creative new idea. Try this way of formulating the new idea. Be critical of that word, of that phrase. Try this other word, this better phrase. Be willing to clarify and clarify, to write down the point and to revise the actual wording. Grant yourself the luxury of being unsatisfied with the actual wording. Grant yourself the luxury of taking plenty of time to keep clarifying the written statement until it is just right. Stop. Return later and see if you are as satisfied. Grant yourself the luxury of being dissatisfied enough to try again and again until the statement is beautifully clear.

There are at least two reasons for all this careful clarification. One is that you will produce a very clear statement of your creative idea. The second reason is that the very effort to clarify the creative idea usually gives rise to a second wave of creative ideas that arise as you are working hard at clarifying the first creative idea. You are hard at work clarifying the initial creative idea, and that effort can yield the second wave of creative new ideas. This is the creative payoff or bonus of clarifying the initial creative idea.

2. Look for creative alternatives to seeing it as a problem with this kind of solution

When you label or define something as a problem, it is often almost automatic that the labeled or defined problem contains its own built-in solution. If this is what the problem is, then that must be the solution, the resolution of the problem, the valued direction of change. Here are some kinds of labeled or defined problems and the virtually built-in solutions:

(a) It is a problem because the person does not have or show a normal amount or degree of it. Either the person has or shows too little of it, and that makes it a problem, or the person has or shows too much of it, and that makes it a problem. It is either hyper-normal or hypo-normal, too strong or too weak, too much or too little. Therefore, it is a problem, and the solution is for the person to have or show a normal degree of it, to reach or return to a normal range of it.

She has a sexual desire that is too strong, too frequent, or she has too little sexual desire, it is too infrequent. She should instead have a normal degree and frequency of sexual desire. His following of rules is too rigid, too inflexible, he is too rule-directed; or he does not follow rules enough, he shows too little abiding by rules. He should instead have a normal degree of abiding by and following rules. She is much too aggressive, or she has much too little aggression. She needs to have a normal degree of aggressiveness.

He is much too competitive, or he lacks a sense of normal

competitiveness. He needs to have a normal degree of competitiveness. She craves food too much, or she lacks the ordinary appetite for food. She needs to have a normal desire for food. He is too dependent, or he is too independent. He needs to be in the normal range of dependence and independence. She is much too committed, much too dedicated and devoted, or she has far too little, virtually no indication of, dedication, devotion and commitment. She should have a normal degree of this quality. He is much too open, unconstrained, lacking normal control, spontaneous, expressive, or he is much too controlled, unexpressive, contained. He should be in the normal range of control and expressiveness.

(b) It is a problem because it is a sign, an indication, a symptom of a pathology, a maladjustment, a mental illness or disorder, something amiss, something that is wrong. The problem has a label, a category, a name. The person has a borderline personality, an attention deficit hyperactivity disorder, a sibling rivalry problem, a panic disorder, a compulsive disorder, an anger management problem, an abusive personality, a dependency problem.

If this is the problem, the direction of change is that the person is no longer to be pathological, maladjusted, mentally ill, mentally disordered. The explicit direction of change is built into the label. Accordingly, the person is no longer to have a borderline personality, an attention deficit hyperactivity disorder, a sibling rivalry problem, and so on.

(c) It is a problem because there is pain, an unhappy, unpleasant, hurtful state or condition or feeling. The person has a painful feeling of loneliness, depression, guilt, anger, rejection, jealousy, chaos, confusion, helplessness, grief, dread, anxiety.

If the person is judged as having some sort of painful bad feeling, the built-in direction of change is toward having much less of the painful bad feeling, or no longer being plagued by it, or its no longer being so common or so painful. Accordingly, the name of the problem also contains the direction of change. Take this pill, carry out this program, be in this therapy, and your loneliness is gone, there is no more depression, the guilt is diffused, you will not feel so rejected, and so on.

The problem is that none of these three scenarios has much likelihood of helping you to come up with creative new ideas. Each is a way of identifying the problem, complete with its own built-in direction of change. Coming up with creative new ideas is defeated both in the way the problem is labeled and in its automatically producing what to do about the problem. Coming up with creative ideas is helped by looking for creative alternatives both to the way the problem is identified and to the direction of change.

One guideline is to try to answer this question: what can be a creative alternative to seeing that as a problem to be fixed? What is a creative alternative to describing it as a problem of abnormally too much or too little; as a problem of something pathologically wrong, mentally disordered; or as a painful bad feeling or state? Study what is ordinarily called the problem to see whether there is any creative alternative way of making sense of and describing what you are making sense of and describing.

A second guideline is to try to answer this other question: what can be a creative alternative to what is ordinarily done to fix what is regarded as the problem? What is a creative alternative to bringing the person to a normal range of functioning; to aiming at curing or reducing the pathology or the mental illness or disorder; to getting rid of or reducing the painful bad feeling? Study the direction of change to identify some creative alternative.

Coming up with creative new ideas can occur in that sensitive and important time when you identify what you are to study, when you are defining the problem you are to study. Creative new ideas can come before you go ahead and label what you study, before you give it a name, before you put it into some category, before you call it whatever you call it. This can be a magnificently creative few moments when you know how to use these moments to come up with creative new ideas.

The time that is on his mind is last night when he and his wife are sitting in the living room, he comes up with a few suggestions about what he would like for dinner, she gives him 'that look', he feels the rage boiling inside, immediately ejects out of his chair, marches out of the living room, face livid with rage, and slams the door as he explodes out of the house. Even before he finishes his description of what happened, some of the people watching the videotape have already identified and labeled a 'problem' of poor control of aggression, an anger management problem, over-reactivity, a rage reaction, a problem of a violent personality, and others have identified and labeled a 'problem' of male abusiveness, gender inequality, a communication problem, female empowerment problem, a female–male role relationship problem, a couples problem.

It can make sense to weigh up the different versions of the problem, and perhaps to select one description and its built-in direction of change, the solution to the problem, the goal or valued outcome. On the other hand, suppose that we can be ready and willing to look for a creative alternative to seeing something as a problem, to labeling something as this or that kind of problem, and to unfolding the built-in solution or valued direction of change. What can we do? There can be at least two ways of arriving at a creative alternative:

(a) What is a creative alternative to seeing 'that' and to labeling 'that' as some kind of a problem? His description of the events lends itself so nicely to identifying what happened as a problem and to labeling what happened as a particular kind of problem. Is there some other, perhaps creative, way of making sense of what he is describing?

For example, in that whole scenario, is there some tiny instant when the feeling in him was most intense, saturating, highest? Is there something about that entire scenario that still lingers with him, that is still compelling, that is still on his mind? Actually, the answer is yes. It was that momentary look on her face and, quite surprisingly, the heightened feeling was not anger, not violence, not rage. He did not even feel as if he were dumb, boorish, foolish. What he actually felt was rattled, confused, bewildered, like a little boy. Her look was not one of annoyance or anger. It was a look of amusement, fondness, a look of 'you are such a little boy'.

Truthfully, her look stayed with him from then on. He sampled what it was like to have that look when he looked in the mirror that morning while he was shaving, and he even tried it on for size during safe moments of the committee meeting at work later that day. For him, the look both felt and said, 'But you must be jesting ... You are such a little boy ... I look upon you with fondness, but of course I know better than anyone ... Now let us think carefully about what you just said, little fellow ...'

It can make good sense to make sense of what he is saying in terms of some sort of problem, and to label the problem the way it fits to label the problem. However, creative possibilities can be opened up by looking for some other way of making sense of what he is saying, by looking for and finding some creative alternative to seeing 'that' through the mind-set of looking for and finding problems.

(b) Try to answer this question: what is a creative alternative to the more or less standard solution to the problem, the common way of fixing the problem, the ordinary direction of change, the ordinary goal or outcome? Can there be a creative alternative to, for example, gaining better control over aggressive impulses, reducing the strength of the inner rage, being better able to read the aggressive cues, treating his male abusiveness, increasing female empowerment, enabling better male–female communication?

Suppose that looking for a creative alternative helps you to come up with these kinds of possibilities. The fellow can ask his wife to show him how to have that special 'look'. She agrees, and they stand in front of the mirror, with her as the teacher and he as the student, learning that look. Or, another alternative direction of change or goal, what else might he do to undergo that pleasant sense of playful superiority, of fond amusement at what the other is doing, of parental acceptance of the childishness of others?

Creative ideas can come when you look for creative alternatives to a mind-set of seeing something as a problem, to labeling the problem this way or that way, and to coming up with the built-in solution or way out or outcome of the problem. Letting go of this mind-set and looking for an alternative mind-set can offer creative possibilities.

3. The creative phases of most research occur before and after doing the research

Actually carrying out a piece of research almost requires that the researcher has determined the research question or hypothesis, and the design and methodology for what to study, what the research is aimed at accomplishing, its purposes and goals, how to go about the study, how to do the actual work, how to obtain the data, and how to make sense of the findings (Mahrer, 2004a). All of this can call for a great deal of careful thinking and work, yet if creative thinking is to take place, it can generally take place before the researcher actually carries out the study. Although doing the actual research can be accompanied by some creative thinking, the ceiling is relatively low. Doing the actual study is not especially conducive to creative thinking.

Even researchers who beat the drum on behalf of creative thinking, creative research methodologies and designs (e.g. Giorgi, 1986; Glazer and Strauss, 1967; Henwood and Pidgeon, 1993; Maslow, 1971) testify that the actual carrying out of the study is much more a matter of careful work, systematic procedures, precision and objectivity than it is the place for creative research thinking and the formulation of creative new ideas.

Nor are most researchers especially schooled or seasoned in the creative aspects of research. What most researchers do, and what most researchers are trained to do, is to find some research topic, to have some aim or purpose for the research, to know what designs and methodologies to use, to be able to call upon and to use the appropriate statistics, and to portray the findings in some acceptable matrix or table or statistics or graph. Then the researcher tends to go on to the next study.

What is typically downplayed or de-emphasized or omitted is doing some solid creative thinking. This can take place before and after the actual study is done. Or the researcher can go through the 'before' phase of research and the 'after' phase without paying much attention to using these phases for creative thinking.

3.1 Researchers commonly ignore the creative before and after phases of research

It can be easy for the researcher to start from some idea that the researcher already has, some idea that the researcher has had around lately, some pet notion, some personal idea, some idea that perhaps is in fashion or is in competition with some rival idea. This way of arriving at what to study does not especially highlight creativity.

The researcher can do the study to show that what the researcher believes is true is indeed true. The aim is to bolster what the researcher believes, to confirm or strengthen what the researcher believes. The aim is to show that what the researcher believes is supported by empirical evidence, by real research.

The researcher's work starts with putting this idea into some testable form. Spell out what you believe is true, and then try to put it into the form of a research hypothesis, a testable hypothesis. Often, this takes some creativity, but not much (Mahrer, 1988; Weimer, 1979).

When the findings are in, creativity can be bypassed by either simply proclaiming that the hypothesis was confirmed, or not, or finding some culprit if the findings were unfriendly. Blame the design or methodology, the sample, the actual subjects, the statistics, the research associates, something that inadvertently interfered with the data collection, something that can be resolved for the next part of the study. This is excuse-making, blame avoidance. But it is not an especially noble example of solid creative thinking.

3.2 Here are some ways of engaging in creative thinking in the 'before' phase of research

In the before phase, the researcher clarifies what is to be studied and how to go about studying it. Here are some ways of engaging in creative thinking in this before phase.

(a) Most researchers start with an idea of the topic that is to be studied. The researcher is going to study the therapist–client relationship or treatment of psychotics or whether psychotherapy is better than pills in treating this or that mental disorder. In general, once the topic is selected, most researchers can have a choice of why they are doing the research, what they are after. Reichenbach (1938) distinguished between knowledge gained from a context or purpose of discovery and that gained from a context or purpose of confirmation. Even before the research is done, in this first phase, the researcher is geared toward discovery, exploring unexplored territory, discovering new knowledge, or the researcher is geared toward confirming what the researcher already believes is true. 'Typically, the discovery context is the source for our concepts and hypotheses, and the justification context is the warrant for their confirmation or their disconfirmation' (Borgen, 1992: 113). First there is a wisp of discovery, and then the researcher goes about the common confirmation or disconfirmation.

Creative thinking is brought into play, in this before phase, to the extent that the researcher sets out to do research in order to discover. The invitation is to do 'discovery-oriented research' (Mahrer, 1985, 1988, 1996a, 1996b, 2004a; Mahrer and Boulet, 1999). Consider learning about and getting into the mind-set of discovery-oriented research. Creative thinking is brought into play when the researcher gets into the discovery-oriented mind-set in this before phase of research.

(b) Once you are drawn toward some topic, some target of study, go ahead and engage in creative thinking. This is the place. Take plenty of time to think about what the research will aim at, try to achieve. Ruminate about the issue, the problem, the topic. Think. Think creatively. Consider creative possibilities. Put creative possibilities on the table. Study them carefully with an eye to seeing which possibilities are truly creative

Keep going until you arrive at a solution, an answer, a creative possibility. Whatever way you call upon your own creative thinking, do so, and wait until you come up with an idea that is exciting, research-worthy, inviting, inspiring, creative. Then you can go ahead with the research.

(c) Once you have a reasonably considered idea of what you want your research to do, of the purpose or aim of your research, the typical next step is to frame a research question or an hypothesis. This can be hard to do because there are not many generally accepted guidelines for how to go from the general purpose or aim to the more specific one (Hoshmand, 1989). Perhaps a major guideline is to frame the research question or hypothesis in a way that is testable. That is good enough, but creative thinking can add another guideline.

Frame your hypothesis in a way that allows it to be refuted, falsified, shown to be wrong. Popper (1972a, 1972b, 1980) argued on behalf of this guideline, but he did so mainly on straight research grounds, that is, in terms of research rigor and carefulness. His guideline is also in accord with engaging in some creative thinking before the actual research is carried out. For one thing, you are engaging in creative thinking when you force yourself to figure out what kind of design and methodology for this particular study can actually refute and falsify the hypothesis. In addition, the very act of considering that your hypothesis just may be wrong, may be refuted and falsified, is a small but mighty step toward thinking in new ways. You have thereby entered the doorway of creative thinking. If your hypothesis might be wrong, refuted, falsified, you are in the exciting world of other possibilities, of creative new thinking. Go ahead. Do your best to work out how your hypothesis might be shown to be wrong, refuted, falsified. You have backed through the doorway of creative new thinking.

3.3 Here are some ways of engaging in creative thinking in the 'after' phase of research

You have carried out the study. You have obtained findings. You are now ready to frame the results, the findings. You can do this after phase of research in ways that minimize or that can allow for a real possibility of creative thinking. Here are some ways of calling on some creative thinking in the final phase of most research.

Suppose that you are doing a study that looks at a particular component of the therapist–client alliance and wants to see whether that component plays a relatively large part in the outcome. Or suppose you are looking at a number of items that might correspond with early drop-out from therapy. Or suppose that you are seeing whether your favorite intervention is effective in treating this mental disorder. There are at least three ways in which you can do some creative thinking in the after phase of your study, when the findings are in.

(a) Whether your findings are friendly or unfriendly, pay some attention to your findings, or those parts of the findings, that are unexpected, surprising, hard to make sense of, exceptional, inexplicable, simply don't seem to fit. These may be the main findings or, perhaps more commonly, they are little pieces or bits that depart from the main findings, the exceptions. They are extraordinary. Make sure that you take a close look at these unexpected and inexplicable findings. Don't incorporate them into the main findings. Don't overlook them as unfitting noise.

Do your best to allow these exceptional or inexplicable findings to spark creative thinking. Allow them to be the windows into something new, something different from the main findings. Here is where you could and should allow creative thinking to come into play. In addition to reporting and discussing the main findings, include a few paragraphs or so on the creative opportunities offered by these unusual, exceptional, inexplicable findings.

(b) Whether your findings are friendly or unfriendly, you can discuss the findings and their implications in a way that stays relatively close to the data and the actual findings. In other words, you can be reasonably careful and conservative in reporting and discussing the findings.

In addition to the conservative discussion of the findings and their implications, you could and should go a step further. You can still be reasonable and logical, but you can use reason and logic to go further into the more creative meanings and implications of your findings. Put on your creative cap and let yourself dip into the creative possibilities, the creative speculations, the more risky meanings and implications of the findings. In other words, consider having both a more conservative and a more creative discussion of the meanings and implications of your findings.

(c) The findings may be unfriendly, perhaps because they do not confirm what you wanted to confirm, or perhaps because they are not solid or clear enough to allow solid and clear conclusions. The ordinary course is to blame things such as unforseen problems with the subjects, design and methodology problems, measurement problems, statistical problems, problems in the framing of the testable hypotheses, and so on.

In addition, such unfriendly findings may be taken at face value, and you can use the findings to open up creative possibilities. If these are the findings, what are the creative possibilities in accepting these findings? Given these findings, let these findings be the touchstone for creative thinking. Creatively speculate. Be creative in thinking about what these obtained findings might mean. Try to consider the creative possibilities arising out of the findings that you did find.

Most researchers go through a before phase in which they decide on the topic, find an hypothesis, select an appropriate design and methodology. Then they carry out the research and they have some data to look at. In the after phase, the researcher makes sense of the data and discusses the findings. For researchers interested in dipping into some creative thinking, the guidelines show how this can be done especially in the before and after phases of the research. The guidelines need not interfere with what the researcher might ordinarily do. They can merely add a little creative wrinkle in the before and after phases that the researcher will ordinarily go through in any case. In other words, the creative guidelines can be friendly.

4. Creative ideas can come from identifying and trying to solve the 'breakthrough problems'

Many fields know what is meant by 'breakthrough problems', have generally acknowledged ideas of what the breakthrough problems are in that particular field, know the state of efforts to solve those problems. If a theoretician or a researcher seeks to address a breakthrough problem, it is not too difficult to have some idea of what they are in fields such as genetics, biochemistry, cellular medicine, chemical engineering, microbiology, solid state theory, mathematical physics, microwave circuitry, satellite communication, fluid mechanics, spatial data analysis, biophysics. Things are likely to be different if a researcher sets out to try to solve a breakthrough problem in the field of psychotherapy. Picture a doctoral student or a seasoned researcher looking for a list of the breakthrough problems in the field of psychotherapy. Picture a doctoral student asking her supervisor, or a seasoned researcher asking the granting agency or his colleagues, what the current breakthrough problems are in the field of psychotherapy. It is hard to picture the researcher being handed a helpful list of what the field of psychotherapy regards as its breakthrough problems. It is more likely that neither the researcher nor those the researcher might talk with have a very clear idea of what might be meant by 'breakthrough problems' in the field of psychotherapy.

4.1 What is a useful meaning of 'breakthrough problems'?
If we were in many fields of science, other than the field of psychotherapy, it is likely that there would be a substantial idea of what might be meant by 'breakthrough problems'. But in the field of psychotherapy, not only would many colleagues have little or no picture of what might be referred to as breakthrough problems, but even the notion of breakthrough problems would probably be rather foreign.

Breakthrough problems are (a) the big problems, the ones that are challengingly unsolved; (b) the problems that are generally acknowledged by much of the field, rather than coming from and pertaining mainly to just a few schools or approaches; and (c) the problems whose solutions would genuinely qualify as breakthroughs, in that they would be likely to lead to substantial advances in the field, some of which may be spelled out and some of which may be hard to predict.

4.2 The field of psychotherapy doesn't put much attention on breakthrough problems or even on the idea of breakthrough problems
There are at least a few considerations that help make such a case. One

consideration is that the field of psychotherapy is not especially forthcoming with regard to lists of breakthrough problems. We have few lists that include psychotherapy's equivalent of how to achieve cold fusion, whether the universe is expanding or shrinking, how life began on earth. I found virtually no such lists when I looked for material in my amateur, provisional attempts to identify the embarrassing problems, the revolutionary basic issues, or the actual breakthrough problems in the field of psychotherapy (Mahrer, 1997a, 1999, 2000a).

A second consideration is that the field of psychotherapy has easy ways of dispensing with what might otherwise loom as a breakthrough problem. As a result, breakthrough problems have almost no chance of surviving in the field of psychotherapy.

(a) Name a problem. The field has a solution. Ask an important question. The field has ready answers. The field produces solutions and answers with the ease of a popcorn popper. We have solutions and answers to problems and questions that have not even taken shape.

(b) Instead of acknowledging a problem as a breakthrough problem, the field deprives a problem of its status as a problem by placing it under some label, topic. The field gives the problem a label, and that takes care of that. We understand that; it is tension reduction, primary attachment, social learning, altruism, object cathexis, modeling, self-actualization, ambivalence, salutogenesis, construct permeability, partial reinforcement. No problem.

(c) Instead of letting a breakthrough problem be, the ploy is to deprive it of its breakthrough status by cavalierly waving to the extensive writings of some prolific writer and thinker. This easily gives the impression that the breakthrough problem is familiar, is taken care of, is well-discussed, is resolved. See the writings of Piaget, Brunner, Maslow, Watson, Rogers, Allport, Skinner, Mowrer, Kohut, or many others.

(d) A breakthrough problem can be deprived of its status as a breakthrough problem by being converted from something that can actually be accomplished to something that is a long-range goal, perhaps something that might be realized in a century or more. For example, it might qualify as a breakthrough problem if everyone in the world recited these words, or drank this potion, and the consequence was that in three days there was world peace. This breakthrough problem would lose much of its breakthrough standing if it were converted into a kind of long-range, ultimate goal. Some day we do hope to achieve world peace. Wouldn't that be nice? Now it is a long-range goal, no longer a breakthrough problem.

(e) A breakthrough problem can be diminished, and lose its breakthrough quality, if its meaning or picture is reduced to being within easy reach. For example, a few thousand years ago, the problem of how to know the heavenly bodies may have consisted of how to provide reasonable predictions of eclipses or explanations of planetary movements that were in accord with the religious canons and dictums. On the other hand, the problem might have achieved breakthrough status if the meaning or picture of the problem included black holes, other galaxies, and how to actually land a spacecraft on faraway planets.

The net result is that the field of psychotherapy has little demonstrated regard for identifying its own breakthrough problems.

4.3 A field that can acknowledge breakthrough problems is a field that can welcome creative thinking

Picture psychotherapists who are engaged in assembling a list of the breakthrough problems in the field. Picture that these psychotherapists slowly assemble and then publish their list, and that other psychotherapists study the list. Creative thinking is fostered in the very efforts to search the literature for breakthrough problems, to keep an eye open for previously published lists. The published list or lists virtually cry out for creative thinking to help solve these breakthrough problems.

In contrast, a field that seems to have little or no familiarity with breakthrough problems is likely to be a field with a low ceiling on creative thinking. Picture a field where there is little or no serious consideration of the idea of breakthrough problems. There are virtually no conferences on the topic, or symposia, or journal articles. There are no lists of breakthrough problems, no discussion of recent progress toward solutions. If a field is reluctant to accept the idea of breakthrough problems, my impression is that the field is reluctant to use this way to engage in whole-hearted creative thinking.

4.4 What are some 'breakthrough problems' according to the experiential perspective?

These breakthrough problems come from the experiential approach, and they are limited to the subject matter of experiential psychology and experiential psychotherapy. These are not breakthrough problems in Jungian psychology or in cognitive psychology. They are not breakthrough problems for the field of psychotherapy.

For many of these breakthrough problems, there are provisional experiential answers. However, it seems fairly clear that the answers are conspicuously provisional, that there is plenty of room for far better answers, and that the problems remain breakthrough problems in and for experiential psychology and psychotherapy.

How can a person discover what lies deeper inside? How can we go deeper and deeper inside the person, discover the deeper worlds that may lie deep inside the person? The experiential approach has a way of going into and exploring a deeper world of potentials for experiencing. Does it make sense to conceive of other inner worlds, of still deeper worlds inside? In the experiential system, what is deeper consists of potentials for experiencing, possibilities for experiencing that lie deep within this person. Could there be other things in other deeper worlds inside the person?

How can a person become the person that the person can become? This breakthrough problem requires a belief that there is a person that the person can become. The experiential model is based on just such a belief. (a) Relationships between potentials for experiencing can become integrative, friendly, accepting, welcoming. (b) Deeper potentials for experiencing can become operating potentials for experiencing. That is, what is deeper inside the person can become integral new parts of an integral new person. When these two, back-to-back changes occur well enough and far enough, the person can be said to become the person that the person can become.

The breakthrough problem is how to achieve this magnificent change. I have two amateur solutions, one when the person is working with an experiential teacher (Mahrer, 1996/2004), and one when the person is working with oneself (Mahrer, 2002b). But I believe there is plenty of room for much better solutions to this breakthrough problem.

How can a person become an 'optimal' person? In order for this to rank as a breakthrough problem, it is almost necessary that there be a meaning or picture of an optimal person or an 'optimal state', and that this state be different from, perhaps much more than, what a person can become. In the experiential system, there is such a meaning or picture of an optimal state, and the breakthrough problem is how a person can achieve this magnificent state.

How can magnificent, deep-seated, transformational in-session changes last for hours, days, weeks, and years? In most experiential sessions, two changes can be achieved. One is that the person can transform into a qualitatively new person. What is deeper inside can become an integral part of the radical new person that the person becomes. The person metamorphoses into a whole new person. A second magnificent in-session change is that painful scenes, and the painful feelings in those painful scenes, simply wash away when the person transforms into becoming the whole new person that the person is capable of becoming. Those painful scenes are no longer a part of the new person and the new person's personal world. The painful feelings in those painful scenes are gone, over with, dissipated.

But here is the problem. These magnificent, transformational changes can occur in most experiential sessions. They can last for 10–50 minutes or so, in a session that lasts for perhaps 90–120 minutes or more. But they do not always last till the end of the session. They do not always last for an hour after the session, nor for a few days or weeks or months or years after the session. What can be done to help these wonderful changes last a while? That is a breakthrough problem in experiential psychotherapy.

How can a person be freed of bad, unpleasant, hurtful feelings that (a) are relatively mild, rather than intense and powerful; (b) seem to occur in many or most situations, rather than being linked to or found in particular situations; (c) seem to be almost an intrinsic part of the person in that the bad feelings are here almost any time and every time; and (d) seem to be part of the very character of the person as far back as the person can remember? Here are some examples of such lifelong, mild, bad feelings that seem part of the very fabric of who and what the person has been and is (Mahrer, Boulet and Robson, 1998):

- feeling like a loser, second rate, unable to succeed, not good enough;
- feeling mildly tense, worried, nervous, fretful, agitated;
- feeling alone, lonely, always by yourself, never really close;
- feeling out of place, not fitting in, not belonging;
- feeling suspicious, distrustful, not able to entrust yourself;
- feeling guilty, inexcusable, blamable, culpable, at fault;
- feeling resentful, critical, picky, grumbling, fault-finding;
- feeling no one really cares, appreciates, wants, loves you;
- feeling gloomy, depressed, what's the use;
- feeling vulnerable, exposed, defenseless, able to be hurt;
- feeling unsure, uncertain, mixed up, confused, unconfident;
- feeling that something bad is imminent, going to happen;
- feeling there is something not quite right, abnormal, twisted, wrong, awful, about you.

These lifelong, mild, bad feelings seem almost impervious to ordinary life changes, to psychotherapy. They seem to fall outside the targets of most psychotherapies. They seem so intrinsic to the person that getting at them directly may well threaten the very existence of the person. Even though these lifelong, mild, bad feelings are not dramatic, how to become free of them is a deserving breakthrough problem.

Where does 'personality' come from in the first place? What are the origins of the person that the person is? The problem is not especially well solved by citing general factors or variables such as a combination of genetics and environment. The problem is perhaps solved, within the experiential system at least, when (a) we are able to produce or help bring about an infant, a child, an adult who is impressively close to what the experiential system regards as an integrated and actualized person, the fundamental stuff of what this person can become, or (b) we can use the solution to help make a truly impressive change, for example, in experiential sessions, either by the client oneself or with the help of an experiential psychotherapist.

What kind of breakthrough device could help accomplish these breakthrough results? Of course science has relied on a continuous flow of grand inventions, wonderful new technologies and clever devices. These are a foundation of science. Breakthrough new devices are essential to the advancement of science.

> With telescopes, microscopes, spectroscopes, Geiger counters, lie detectors, and the thousands of other contrivances of modern science we manage to amplify our senses and thus to open up avenues of at least indirect access to the worlds of the very distant, the very large, the extremely small, or the disguised and concealed. (Feigl, 1953: 13)

Creative new ideas can come about in the course of (a) identifying what some device could do, could provide, could be for; (b) identifying what the device might consist of, work like, be like; and (c) identifying what we might find or be able to do if we had such a device. Asking and trying to answer these kinds of questions is putting yourself in a position of readiness to have creative new ideas.

Here are some examples of the kinds of practical devices that could be breakthrough devices in and for experiential sessions: (a) It is so hard to find rooms that are conducive to experiential sessions. Quite simply, what is needed is some way of creating a truly sound-proofed room or zone in which the person can have an experiential session. With the new device, the person can make a great deal of noise, and the noise would not be heard outside the 'cone of silence', the sound-proofed zone, nor would the person hear noise from outside. (b) The new device would be a 'dream recorder'. Turn it on before you fall asleep. When you wake up, you use the dream recorder to see and hear and to be in the dream you were in when you were dreaming. (c) The new device is a feeling indicator. It can locate where the feelings are occurring in your body, and it can measure the strength of feelings, whether the strength is increasing or decreasing. (d) The special new device is a virtual reality room. By pushing the right buttons, you can create or recreate a particular scene, situation, world. The virtual reality may be from past scenes or from fantasy. Push the right buttons and you are having brandy with the very special other person, just the two of you, enjoying being with one another.

These are some of the breakthrough problems in the experiential system. Creative thinking can be helped to occur in the search for (a) the naming and identification of breakthrough problems within particular approaches or in the general field of psychotherapy itself, and (b) the actual solutions to the breakthrough problems. First ask, 'What are the breakthrough problems?' Then ask, 'What are the solutions to the breakthrough problems?' Asking and answering these questions can help set the stage for creative thinking.

CHAPTER 6

Develop the Idea into a Creative New Idea

When you are working at something, the chances are that you will come up with some idea. You are figuring out how to work with this supervisee, how to make sense of these research findings, what your own notion is about this topic you are reading about, how to understand what happened in the therapy session, what can be done with regard to this ethical issue, what to say in the discussion section, how to organize this new program, how to solve the issue on the committee agenda, where to look in seeking the cause of this client's problem. You have lots of ideas in the course of doing what you do as a psychotherapist who is a practitioner or teacher or supervisor or researcher or theorist or committee member or administrator.

Your idea may be rather ordinary, simple, or it might be extraordinary, complex. It may be a fair idea or a brilliant idea. It may bear upon this little problem or issue you are working on, or it may have broader and far more comprehensive implications. It may be somewhat familiar to you, or it may be a new idea for you. It may be your idea, or it may belong to some other person or to these other groups, although the idea is helpful in whatever you are trying to achieve. It may be quite familiar in the general field, or it may be somewhat distinctive. It may stay with you for a while, or it may evaporate as soon as you use it in whatever you are busy doing.

There is another way of using the ideas that come to you, that are part of what you do in your work. You can develop an idea into a creative new idea. This is another way of using the ideas you have. It is an uncommon way of using your flow of ideas. The very idea of using ideas this way is usually a whole new idea. You probably have little or no experience of seeing an idea as something you can work on, you can fashion and build, you can develop into a creative new idea. This chapter says that it is possible to start with one of those ideas that you have and to develop it into a whole new, creatively new idea.

The notion is rather simple. Start with an idea and use one of these ways to develop the idea into a creative new idea. Although the notion seems rather simple, it can take a fair amount of study and understanding to be able to develop an idea into a creative new idea. As you consider what is helpful to know, you can lose sight of how all of this connects with the simple notion of developing an idea into a creative new idea. You may feel sidetracked or lost. Or you can be excited at seeing how to start with an idea and how to use these particular ways to develop the idea into a creative new idea.

Are you interested? Would you like to do this? How does the idea strike you? If there is even a gleam of interest, the purpose of this chapter is to show you how. There are ways to start with an idea and to help develop it into a creative new idea. The rest of the chapter consists of some specific ways to develop an idea into a creative new idea.

1. Pump up an idea until it bumps into a generally accepted, big-time truth

Start with some idea. Then keep pumping it up bigger and bigger until it bumps into some generally accepted truth. You are now in the world of creative new ideas.

Start with some observation, a statement of truth, a finding from a study. Here are some ideas to start with: (a) I can beat my opponent in the amateur boxing match. (b) During the session with the client, I thought there was blood coming from my right nostril, but there was no blood. (c) The students were quite sure they were right, although there was essentially no evidence to justify their certainty. (d) The client went through an impressive change, in the session, and this was followed by a new way of understanding how he had always thought about his mother and his relationships with his previous two wives. (e) With the therapist's attention fully on what the client was attending to, the therapist felt what the client was feeling.

How can you go about pumping up your idea, making it bigger and broader? You can enlarge the focus or target or subject of the idea. In the original idea, your focus was on a particular opponent in the forthcoming amateur boxing match. You can enlarge the idea by extending the focus outward, enlarging the focus: 'I can beat any opponent in amateur boxing'. You can also enlarge the idea by enlarging the context. In the original statement, the context was amateur boxing. Here is one enlargement of context: 'I can beat any opponent in professional boxing.' Now keep enlarging both the focus and the context. You can arrive at this idea: 'I am better than everybody at everything!'

With each enlargement, there can be a part of you that reacts with hearty and increasingly strong doubt, skepticism, disbelief. 'That is rather silly ... That is very unlikely ... That is ridiculous! ... You are out of your mind!' The more you pumped up the original idea, the more you bumped up against bigger and bigger truths: 'The truth is that you cannot beat any opponent in amateur boxing. That is silly ... The truth is that you cannot beat any opponent in professional boxing. That is ridiculous ... The truth is that you are not better than everybody at everything. You really have lost your mind.'

Pumping up the little idea into a much bigger and broader idea is neither a matter of induction nor deduction. Nor is it especially a matter of careful logical reasoning. It is more what Kantor calls 'autistic extrapolation' that can rise up and bump into generally accepted truths: 'It is no great task to differentiate between extrapolation which generates and furthers our contacts with specific essential things, and extrapolation consisting of autistic constructions which implement the creation of ultimates and absolutes' (Kantor, 1950: 15). Keep pumping up the idea until it bumps up against an established ultimate and absolute, some generally accepted truth, some general law, canon, dictum, empirically confirmed statement of knowledge.

Start with some idea, such as any of those mentioned earlier, or an observation such as this: 'In the initial session, the client was consistently on the verge of falling apart about her husband having just left after 17 years of marriage; I told her to go ahead and let herself fall apart; she did and she seemed a whole different person!' Here are some ways of pumping up this little observation, this little idea, so that it becomes a big idea, bumps into a generally accepted truth or clinical practice or dictum, and flowers into a creative new idea:

(a) The generally accepted truth is that in initial sessions the therapist is to identify the presenting complaint, get a case history, do an assessment or evaluation. However, you have pumpedup your little observation until it bumps up against this generally accepted truth and is bathed in creative thinking as it emerges as this big idea: the initial session can be a context for as deep, as broad and as significant a change as the person and the therapist are ready and able to help bring about. In other words, initial sessions can be especially ready and opportune for important changes. Using initial sessions in the standard, ordinary ways can block and prevent chances to enable important changes in these sessions.

(b) Suppose that you keep pumping up your little observation until it bumps up against this generally accepted clinical truth: significant psychotherapeutic change requires the gradual development of a strong therapist–client relationship and working alliance. Your creative new, enlarged, big idea takes this form: significant personality and psychotherapeutic change can occur without the development or presence of a traditional good therapist–client relationship or working alliance. There can be conditions and methods of helping to bring about significant personal change that do not involve development of what is ordinarily meant by a strong therapist–client relationship. Indeed, the common meaning of a strong therapist–client relationship tends to restrict, limit and truncate the kinds of significant personal changes that can be brought about, and can actively block, prevent and inhibit whole classes of significant personal changes from being achieved.

(c) When you keep pumping up your original little idea, it ends up bumping against the following generally accepted clinical truth: psychotherapeutic change occurs in large part because of the therapist's proper application of therapeutic interventions and treatments. As you keep enlarging your creative little idea, it bumps up against that generally accepted clinical truth and takes the following new creative form: in helping to bring about impressive changes, the role of the therapist can be that of the teacher or accompanying guide who shows the ready and willing person what to do to enable change to occur, rather than the ordinary therapist who applies interventions and treatments to the client.

(d) You keep pumping up your original little idea until it bumps up against this traditionally accepted truth: in psychotherapy, the focus is on the client's mental disorder or related symptoms, presenting complaints or problems. However, pumping up your initial idea leads to this larger creative new idea: in psychotherapy, the focus is on the person's sense of strong feeling, pleasant or unpleasant, rather than on the person's mental disorder or related symptoms, presenting complaints, or problems.

Here is an exercise so that you can see firsthand what it can be like to pump up an idea until it bumps up against a generally accepted big-time truth. Start with the five observations, little ideas, mentioned at the beginning of this section. Keep pumping up each of the five until they bump up against a generally accepted, traditional truth. Then let creativity flow by allowing your pumped-up idea to become a creative new idea.

Sometimes the little idea may not especially be yours. It is one that comes from other fields or has been around in one part of the field of psychotherapy. I have been introduced to many such ideas by appreciating many of the writings in the philosophy of science, and the challenge for me is how to apply these ideas to the field of psychotherapy in a way that allows these ideas to keep enlarging.

For example, in many fields, including psychology, an idea is that an observer can have a substantial effect on what is observed. How can this idea be applied to psychotherapy so as to allow this idea to grow bigger and bigger until it challenges and is challenged by a relatively big, generally accepted truth in the field of psychotherapy? Here is one possibility: therapist observations about clients cannot be trusted because an observer can have a big effect on what the observer observes. Much more than merely a warning for the therapist to 'be careful', the creative clash between the enlarged idea and the established canon suggests that perhaps therapist observations are to be set aside, and the search can be for alternative client data that can be more trusted. Can you picture therapist observations being dethroned, set aside? Can you picture a genuine search for alternative data that can be trusted? This is what can happen when you help an idea to get bigger and bigger and to bump up against an established truth.

1.1 Be wary of constraints, constrictions and limitations on pumping up the new idea, on bumping into a generally accepted big-time truth, or on having creative new ideas

It helps if you can be aware of, wary of, and can avoid falling into the usual traps that can effectively sideline you, deflect you, constrain, constrict, limit, block and obstruct you. These traps are clever, exceedingly common, reside in you and in many of your colleagues, and usually require your cooperation.

For example, suppose that there is something compelling and appealing about an idea that an observer can have a substantial effect on what is observed. You take steps toward applying that idea to psychotherapy, toward pumping up that idea, toward having that idea bump up against an established big truth, and toward pursuing the creative possibilities. You go ahead, and are headed toward a dilated new idea: therapist observations about clients cannot be trusted because an observer can have a big effect on what the observer observes. Here are some relatively common deflections, constraints and limitations:

One way is to play the game of pinning a label on the idea. Give it a recognizable name, label. Put the idea in some established category. 'That is called "countertransference"; we know about that.' Such a ploy not only stops the work of giving birth to a creative new idea but also has the advantage of pronouncing the new idea as a familiar old idea, thereby defeating the idea's chances to become a creative new idea: 'We know all about that, so let's talk about something else.'

Another way is to preserve and protect the threatened principle, the established principle. Avoid entering the realm of creative new ideas by patching up the threatened principle. You began with an idea that an observer can have a substantial effect on what is observed. When you applied that idea to the field of psychotherapy, you bumped against a generally established principle: therapists rely on observations and clinical inferences about the client. The looming danger can be letting a creative new idea come forth for example, therapist observations about clients cannot be trusted because an observer can have a big effect on what the observer observes. What can be done to preserve and protect the established principle, and to fend off the looming, menacing, creative new idea?

One answer is to patch up the established principle. Add clauses and auxiliary principles to retain the traditional principle that therapists count on observations and clinical inferences about the client. Patch up the established principle by adding a clause as follows: when there is an adequate therapist–client relationship, therapists can count on their observations and clinical inferences about clients. Add an auxiliary principle: therapists are trained observers who can count on their observations and clinical inferences about clients. Add a different auxiliary principle: because an observer can have a big effect on what the observer observes, the therapist checks out his or her observations and clinical inferences.

The ploy is to modify and revise the established principle in order to keep it around, and to insure against the threat of the creative new idea, namely that therapist observations about clients cannot be trusted because an observer can have a big effect on what the observer observes. Imagine going further and further into the realm of creativity by accepting the idea that therapist observations about clients cannot be trusted. Old basic questions invite new answers. How can therapists know what clients are thinking and feeling? How can therapists gain data about what is occurring in their clients? How can therapists observe clients while minimizing their effects on what the therapists observe?

Suppose that you start with an interesting idea and pump it up until it assumes the following form: learning can occur without reinforcement.

Suppose that, in your way of thinking, this enlarged idea bumps up against a hallowed and established principle, namely the law of effect. How can you avoid considering the creative possibilities of starting with the idea that learning can occur without reinforcement? How can you cling to your traditional principle of the law of effect? The ploy is to add auxiliary and secondary principles to the law of effect. Add a principle of secondary reinforcement (Thorndike, 1932). This enables you to stay with the law of effect, and to resist pulls toward a creative realm with the marquee labeled 'Learning can occur without reinforcement.'

You are pumping up an idea, making it bigger and broader until it can bump up against an established principle. Your pumped-up idea may be: 'learning can occur without reinforcement', or you began with the idea that an observer can have a substantial effect on what is observed, and you pumped it up into this idea: 'therapist observations about clients cannot be trusted because an observer can have a big effect on what the observer observes.' You have arrived at a point where your pumped-up idea can bump up against a generally accepted principle, and here is where creativity enters the picture. You are heading toward coming face to face with a new idea.

A good way of fending off the threat of a creative new idea is to cling to the threatened general principle. Patch it up with conditional clauses and needed auxiliary secondary principles. This ploy can work well.

A third ploy is to point in the general direction of the writings of notable people in the field. Suppose that the pumped-up idea is that therapist observations about clients cannot be trusted because an observer can have a big effect on whatever the observer observes. Instead of going further by allowing this pumped-up idea to bump up against an established principle, and thereby opening the gates to creative thinking, you can puncture the possibility of creative thinking by saying in effect, 'Oh yes, we know all about that', and then point vaguely in the general direction of notable writers in the field. Mention such people as Rogers, Bandura, Erickson, Adler, Strupp, Dreikurs, Allport, Kelly, Freud, Gendlin, Watzlawick, or others. This stops creative thinking in its tracks.

The underlying inference is that because these people knew about and wrote about this notion of therapist observations not being trustworthy, we can stop edging our way toward creative new ideas. Instead of venturing into the zone of creative new ideas, read their writings, even though the ploy does not require specifying a particular reference. 'Allport wrote about that … somewhere … I think … Check it out …'

A fourth ploy is to stop, turn away, go no further, shut down, exit. You have pumped up the idea until it is close to bumping up against a hoary established principle, and, with a few more baby steps, you are on the verge of a creative new idea. Do you have what it takes to bump up against a generally established principle? Do you have what it takes to give birth to a creative new idea that just might threaten, clash with, menace, replace the generally established principle?

Under these explicit conditions, are you willing to risk a direct encounter, a clash, a fight, a confrontation? Do you have the courage to challenge and perhaps set aside the established principle?

If you don't, then one easy ploy, one easy way out, is simply to shut down, stop, turn away, exit, shift your attention to something else. Be nice. Do not fight. Avoid the threat of clashing with the established principle. Do not bump up against it. Do not create a new idea that is going to harm the established principle.

Coming up with creative new ideas is helped by your knowing these various ploys. You can see them coming, and you can dodge them, step out of their way. You know them well enough to avoid being trapped by them. Instead of getting out of the traps, you avoid getting caught by them in the first place.

1.2 Get a creative new idea by applying the pumped-up idea anywhere and everywhere, to all sorts of problems and issues

You can see what big-time truths your pumped-up idea bumps up against. You can also look around to see what other trouble the pumped-up idea can bring about. Apply your pumped-up idea over here and over there. Apply your pumped-up idea to a whole range of problems, issues, questions.

Your 'theory' consists of this one pumped-up idea. It explains everything. It solves a broad range of problems. On almost every issue, here is the good position. It is your version of the single grand idea, 'It is God's will'. That accounts for almost everything. It explains almost everything. Bring up almost any issue or question, and 'It is God's will' can be the position or answer. However, instead of 'It is God's will', the grand, all-purpose idea is your own pumped-up grand idea.

Creativity comes from applying your single grand idea to each problem, issue, question. Creativity lies in using your grand idea here and there, to be your position on this issue, to be your answer to that question, and to be your solution to that problem. No matter what the question, the answer is your single grand idea. No matter what the problem, the solution is your single grand idea.

For example, your pumped-up idea is relatively simple: what is important is the 'experiencing' occurring in the person. So far, this is merely a pumped-up idea. It is not especially producing lots of creative ideas. Here are some ways in which this pumped-up idea can lead to several creative ideas by being applied to a range of issues, problems, and questions:

How and why do 'interpretations' work? What can account for some interpretations working better than others? What is the effective ingredient in interpretations? Suppose that your single grand idea is the answer. 'Experiencing' explains and accounts for how and why interpretations work. Experiencing explains why some interpretations work better than others. The effective ingredient in interpretation is experiencing.

The patient is defensively explaining how surprised he was that he missed his brother's wedding, and how the ceremony was disrupted by the absence of the best man and the ring that the patient had tucked away in his luggage to be certain that he would bring it to the ceremony. The therapist grins and says, 'Well, maybe it was payback time,' and the patient's nervous laughter almost hides his muttered 'Serve him right', hissing out through clenched teeth, accompanied by a burst of cold hard experiencing of anger toward his superior brother.

The creative new idea is that interpretations work because of the experiencing that they help bring about, not by the traditional means of insight and understanding or by their explanatory value. Interpretations can be made better by enabling them to be more effectively linked to producing experiencings, rather than by using proper dosage, timing, readiness, and so on.

Why do clients and patients go to therapists? What accounts for a person seeking out sessions with professional psychotherapists? The common answer is that clients and patients go to therapists for treatment and for relief of their mental problems, their suffering, their worries and concerns, their mental disorders. If the client has bouts of depression, see a therapist. If the client has a sexual dysfunction, problems with grief, an attention deficit disorder, go to a therapist. Clients go to therapists for treatment of mental disorders and for relief of psychic distress and suffering.

You are knocking on creativity's door when you try out your one answer for all issues and problems, namely that what is important is the person's experiencing. Clients and patients do not seek out therapists for treatment of mental disorders or for relief of psychic distress and suffering or anything like that. Instead, people seek out therapists on the basis of experiencing. Playing out this idea can invite bits and pieces of creative thinking. This person seeks out a therapist to have the experiencing of having someone on her side, someone who can defend her, someone who stands between her and the judge who wants to take away her children. This fellow wants to have sessions with the older and attractive psychotherapist, and the underlying experiencing is undergoing safe sexual feelings with an older and attractive woman, especially an educated woman who is a doctor. This other fellow seeks out the right therapist, and the experiencing is an opportunity for the experiencing of being a little boy, dependant on a strong person who allows him to be mixed up, childish, irresponsible, and yet accepted and cared for. She seeks out the right therapist who can be her confidante, her best friend, the one she can tell everything to. With his psychotherapist he undergoes special experiencings of being the little jewel, the precious center of full and unerring attention.

Creative new ideas bubble with life as the experiencing principle replaces the ordinary reasons why clients and patients come to therapy, seek out therapists, have sessions with therapists.

What kinds of data do you trust, consider hard and objective? There are some relatively popular answers. One popular answer is that you can trust research. When the design is a good one and the findings are out to two decimal places, trust research findings. Research makes psychotherapy a science, so trust research. Another popular answer is to trust observable behavior (Bridgman, 1928). If you actually see the patient make a fist and smash her fist against the chair, you can trust the behavior you actually see. A third popular answer is to trust tests, scales, measures. If the test is a good test and the person gets this score, then trust the objective score and its test meaning. A fourth answer is to trust consensus, or near-consensus, among experts, specialists, those with knowledge on the matter, the authorities. If the authorities say it is so, then it is so.

Here is where you turn to your one answer for lots of issues and problems. Suppose that experiencing is the answer to questions about what kinds of data to trust, to rely upon as hard and objective. You know you are drawn toward this woman, and how do you know? You can rely on research findings that say here is the kind of woman you are to be attracted to. You can rely on observable behavior of your smiling at her and walking over to her, and asking whether she would be your wife. You can trust tests and measures about attractiveness. Or you can rely on the massive erection you have, and the experiencing of sheer lust when you are with her.

Once you have a pumped-up idea, you are entering the realm of creative new ideas when you see what it can be like to apply this pumped-up idea to all sorts of problems, issues, questions. In a way, this is a game, but it can be a game with exciting possibilities for creative new ideas.

The game consists of staying with your original creative idea and spawning new creative ideas by applying your original creative idea to any and all issues and questions and problems. Avoid the temptation of acceding to the commonly accepted position or answer or solution. Instead, allow your original creative idea to give rise to a new creative position or answer or solution. For example, behaviorism came up to the commonly accepted issue of rationalism and its associated mentalistic language system and, in a creative stroke, dispensed with that whole mentalistic language system and its mentalistic agencies and entities:

> Behaviorists dealt with Cartesian rationalism by giving it up. Instead of assuming a priori that human beings were rational, they would undertake to discover the facts by observation. While giving rationalism up, they also gave up the logically defective mentalistic language that goes along with it. (Hocutt, 1996: 86)

Here is a test. Start with the following interesting proposition: 'The knowledge of causes implies the knowledge of effects. But the reverse of this proposition is not true. The same effect can be produced by several different causes' (Duhem, 1996: 33). Suppose that you pump up this interesting proposition. The test is to find a number of big problems, issues and questions in the field of psychotherapy. Go ahead. Find one problem, issue or question and enter the zone of creativity by applying that pumped-up proposition. Let yourself come up with daring, bold, far-reaching, perhaps revolutionary new ideas by applying this interesting proposition.

For example, you might start with Duhem's interesting proposition and allow it to spawn further creative ideas by applying it to the common notions and ideas about educating and training psychotherapists, thinking about and doing research, the traditional mind–body problem, issues of where and how personality originates in the first place, how social change comes about, the understanding and use of dreams, what draws psychotherapists and clients to be with and stay with or to end being with one another, and what stamps a conceptual system as a good one.

2. Expand the little idea into the future until it becomes a creative big idea

Start with a little idea. Then insert the little idea into the future, push it into the future, let it expand and grow in the context of the future. For example, start with a little idea that some people can and do undergo their own self-change. Think of some people applying behavior techniques or using guided imagery or studying their own dreams or doing meditation or having their own experiential sessions.

Now put that little idea into the future. Suppose that the idea of people having their own sessions grew and grew over the next 40 years, or over the next 200 years. Suppose that the idea flourished, expanded, grew by leaps and bounds. What you are seeing is the little idea becoming a creative big idea. If the idea became a creative big idea, what might you see 40 or 200 years from now (Mahrer, 2001b)?

Here are some possibilities:

(a) There would be all sorts of technological advances to assist a person in going through their own self-change. For example, the person could have access to a panel of buttons that could create almost any kind of virtual reality. The technology could recreate the scene when the person was four years old and she jumped into the friendly haystack, giggling and laughing. The technology could put the person in a virtual reality scene with a valued and custom-made special companion.

(b) Having one's own sessions of self-change could become quite popular, so that perhaps half the people in most communities would engage in regular self-change sessions, and it would be taught in most school systems.

(c) Suppose that there were a substantial increase in what self-change sessions could help accomplish, and also in ways of accomplishing these changes. A person from today would be bowled over by the wonderful changes that self-change sessions could achieve, and would have to learn the many new self-change skills that had been developed over the past 40 or 200 years.

(d) What might be the consequences of so many people engaging in continuously improved self-change methods and accomplishments? Entering into the possibilities of grand creative ideas, would the consequences include a new era of social change through collective individual self-change? That would seem to be magnificent. Would the consequences include a requiem, a diminishing, a washing away of what is traditionally understood as psychotherapy (Mahrer, 2001b)?

2.1 First arrive at where you are going, then you can see what lies further ahead

Suppose that you are in unfamiliar territory, and there is a mountain ridge in front of you. You don't know what lies beyond that unfamiliar mountain ridge until you reach the ridge. Then you can see what lies beyond.

Expanding the little idea into the future can consist of two steps. The first step brings you to the mountain ridge. It projects you into the future. It enables you to see what it could be like in that particular part of the future. Put yourself on the mountain ridge. Become accustomed to being here on the mountain ridge. You are living and being in the future. Now you are better able to carry out the second step, the creative second step. Look ahead. What do you see beyond this mountain ridge? Having a creative idea entails first being able to become accustomed to the future, and then looking around, looking even further ahead.

Suppose that we had a way that one could undergo deep-seated personal change by oneself. It may be a better form of meditation or a better form of having one's own experiential sessions. Now take the first step. Suppose that almost everyone, 200 years from now, were able to have their own sessions every day or every week or so. Can you actually see this? You are living in a world 200 years ahead, and almost everyone has their own personal sessions. Is this real for you? Have you actually put yourself into this world 200 years from now? Is this world one that is real, understood, familiar? You have completed the first step.

Now look around. What is this world like? What do you see? Do you see people killing other people? Do you see large groups of people hating other large groups of people? Look around and see what you see. This is the second step. This is the truly creative second step.

Suppose that there is, deep inside you, a quality of cherishing, caring for, respecting, appreciating, or a quality or possibility of experiencing riskiness, crossing over boundaries, entering forbidden territories. The first step is to become the deeper quality, to undergo it, to make it an integral part of the whole new person you can become. Then the second step can be to look around you, to see who and what you are now, to see how the world can be for the new person who you are. What kind of world is here when you are the whole new person who can experience cherishing, caring for, respecting, appreciating? What is it like holding your toothbrush, looking at the woman who is here with you, listening to your father tell the story about being drunk for the first time?

Achieving the second step depends upon achieving the first step. You can stay here, and you can try to figure out what it might be like to be the new and different person who listens to your father tell the story. But the chances are that the future situation would be very different if you first became the whole new person and then listened to your father tell the story. The chances are that you would be quite different, your father would be quite different, being with your father would be quite different, and the story would be quite different.

3. Use attacks as doorways to creative new ideas

It is easy to see attacks on your ideas, your theory, your approach, as unpleasant threats. They are out to hurt your idea, to put it down, to see it as flawed, second-rate, in need of fixing. Attacks mean that the attacker does not like your idea, does not see its wonderful worth. Attacks are aimed at hurting your idea and you. Attacks are nasty criticisms, fault-findings. Attacks can damage your precious idea. There is little or nothing virtuous about attacks on your idea. Those who attack your idea are not attacking in order to make you pleased. They attack to do damage to your idea. An attack is a threat. It is an act of war.

It seems to be common to use an attack to defend and protect your idea, your theory, your way of thinking. Stand up for your idea. Show how the attack is misguided, not as serious as it sounds, wrong. Attack the attacker. The attacker doesn't really understand your good idea, your theory. The attacker is attacking your good idea for reasons that are political or personal or professional, rather than solid and grounded. Make sure that the attack is diffused, deflected, turned back on the attacker. Make sure that the attack does little or no harm to your precious idea, your theory.

It seems to be common to believe that an idea or a theory is good if it can withstand attacks, if it can emerge unscathed. If the idea or theory is hurt by the attacks, if it is defeated, then that is proof that the idea or theory is no good.

On the other hand, there can be ways to use attacks as doorways to further ideas, to creative new ideas. Here are a few of these ways:

3.1 Does the attack actually touch a nerve, a serious flaw, weakness, problem? If so, use the attack as an opportunity for creative new ideas

Popper (1972a, 1972b, 1980) shows how you can examine your own theory to see where it falls down, needs work, where it makes big mistakes. He shows how you can do research on your own theory to explicitly see where it can be falsified, refuted, shown to be wrong. Then, according to Popper, you can do some creative thinking to improve your theory, to make it work better, to fix what needs fixing.

Your attacker can actually be on your side by pointing out the flaws in your thinking, the weaknesses and problems in your notions. Be on the

132

lookout for attacks that strike home, that touch your nerve, that you honestly know are accurate. Every so often a criticism is one that you can sense is right. Instead of automatically fighting the attack and the attacker, follow Popper's suggestion. 'This criticism is right! It spots a fatal flaw! I have genuine respect for this accurate criticism.'

Creative thinking can come when you accept the criticism, when you seriously examine the flaw, the weakness, the problem, and then you get to work trying to do something constructive about the matter. How can I fix the flaw? How can I repair the weakness? That truly is a problem, so what can I do about that problem? Answering these kinds of questions can be the springboard to creative new ideas.

3.2 Try to figure out how your ideas can be improved by accepting something of your attacker's ideas

It is quite common for the attacker to say in effect, 'My ideas are better than yours, are superior to yours. You are to give up your ideas and to embrace mine.' In politics, law and religion, it is common to attack by saying, 'My ideas are better than yours, are superior to yours. Give up your ideas and embrace mine.' In the field of psychotherapy, it is quite easy to see most psychotherapists spending a great deal of time saying in effect, 'My ideas are better than yours, are superior to yours. Give up your ideas and embrace mine. Behind most of what I do is the effort to get you to give up your inferior, mixed-up, problem-engendering, inadequate, lesser, pathological, flawed way of thinking, and to accept instead my superior, mentally healthier, better way of thinking' (cf. Anderson and Goolishian, 1992; Derrida, 1978; de Shazer, 1991; Hare-Mustin and Maracek, 1990; Watzlawick, Weakland and Fisch, 1974).

Your attacker wants you to give up your way of thinking and to adopt the way of thinking of your attacker. You may well be inclined to defend and protect your way of thinking. There is little or no creative thinking in either option.

But there is an option that does set the stage for some high-grade creative thinking. This option consists of your trying to figure out how your ideas can be improved by accepting something of your attacker's ideas. Suppose that your attacker's ideas can be allowed to affect your ideas so that, instead of destroying your ideas, the effect is one of adding a creative dash to your own ideas.

Suppose that you hold to a classical psychoanalytic picture of the structure of personality, and your attacker is attacking your idea of an unconscious by aiming at replacing it with the attacker's idea of a growth force, a force for actualization. The attack is tough. Instead of mounting a counter-attack, how can you accept the idea of an actualization growth force so as to open up some creative possibilities for your psychoanalytic theory of the structure of personality? Consider that you come up with at least three possibilities:

(a) You typically think of the unconscious as a kind of force in its own right, exerting its power in relation to other components of personality. Suppose that the unconscious also has a characteristic of a growth force. The unconscious tends to actualize itself. If barriers were removed, obstacles cleared away, the unconscious would be inclined to open itself up, to be 'realized' or 'actualized'.

(b) Suppose that personality contains both an unconscious and a growth force toward actualization. In some people the unconscious is dominant, stronger, and the growth force is inferior, weaker. In some people the case is reversed. Could this picture help to explain some of the dilemmas created by thinking only in terms of the unconscious? Could this picture make for interesting and creative new possibilities for in-session psychoanalytic work?

(c) Suppose that the alien idea of an actualizing growth force is not a threat to the unconscious. Suppose that the addition of a growth force has more to do with accounting for an infant proceeding through psychoanalytic stages of development. The thrust or force that accounts for psychoanalytic development is not only biologically based but also complemented by a psychological growth force.

Instead of defensively resisting or fighting your attacker, see what it can be like to consider accepting the enemy idea so as to open up creative new possibilities.

3.3 Accept the criticism, and use the criticism as a springboard to creative new ideas

Consider that you graciously welcome the criticism. You accept that your notions, your theory or approach, deserve the criticism, not because your ideas are so flawed or inferior but because the criticism is in reaction to something about your ideas that invites the criticism, asks for the criticism, provokes the criticism.

So you ask yourself, 'What is it about my ideas that genuinely warrants the criticism, and, once I find it, how can I use it to generate more creative ideas?' Here are two examples from criticisms of experiential psychotherapy:

First, experiential psychotherapy is criticized as lacking research showing that experiential psychotherapy is good, is effective. Where is the supporting research? There isn't any! The lack of supporting research is a serious problem. What do you have to say? How can you defend yourself?

Suppose that the mind-set is to accept the criticism. Yes, that is true. There is no research to show that experiential psychotherapy is good, is effective. Now let us tiptoe into the pond of creative ideas. Maybe there are other reasons for doing research on psychotherapy. Maybe I am not drawn toward doing research to show my therapy is good, is effective. Maybe I am much more drawn to doing research to discover more and more of what psychotherapy can accomplish, and to discover better and better ways of accomplishing these new and better things (Mahrer, 1985, 1988, 1996a, 1996b, 2004a; Mahrer and Boulet, 1999). The creative idea is to accept that I decline research showing that my therapy is good, and I find that I prefer what I refer to as 'discovery-oriented research'.

Second, experiential psychotherapy is criticized as being deficient in what makes psychotherapy good, successful, and being deficient in what is accepted as standard in most psychotherapies, and also as having features that seem weird, bizarre and virtually counter-therapeutic. Here are some examples. Experiential psychotherapy lacks a proper therapist–client relationship, most of the interventions that are accepted as therapeutically useful, a proper diagnostic assessment procedure, case history material, intake evaluation. Experiential therapists start sessions by screaming and yelling, go through the same steps in each session, close their eyes throughout the sessions and ask clients to do the same, put their attention on whatever the client is attending to instead of attending to the client, have essentially no private inferences.

Instead of trying to defend experiential psychotherapy against these criticisms, suppose that they are welcomed and gracefully accepted. Experiential psychotherapy does lack almost everything that characterizes good and effective psychotherapy. How true. Experiential psychotherapy is deficient in the methods of good and effective psychotherapies. Do not argue. Experiential psychotherapy does not belong among the acknowledged good and effective psychotherapies. Accept this as a sound judgment. Don't fight. Don't argue. Don't grit your teeth and see what can be salvaged from grim reality.

Instead, use these sound and true criticisms as sound and true statements of the state of affairs, and ease your way toward creative new ideas. What can all this mean? How can all this be used as a springboard to creative new ideas?

What comes to you first is a picture of what experiential psychotherapy is for, its aims and goals. You see one goal as the person becoming a whole new person, a qualitatively new person, a radically new person, the altogether new person that the person can become. You see a related goal as the person becoming free of the painful scenes and the painful feelings in the painful scenes. What comes to you next is a picture of experiential psychotherapy as departing substantially from what most other psychotherapies are for, as for something substantially different from what most psychotherapies are for. Finally, with some vibrant excitement, you enter a creative zone, and what comes to you is that you have a relatively clear picture of what most psychotherapies are for, experiential sessions are not for what most psychotherapies are for, and what emerges is that experiential psychotherapy is really not a psychotherapy, is not at all for what most psychotherapies are for.

Either 'psychotherapy' can expand in new and bold ways, to include what experiential psychotherapy is for, or experiential psychotherapy identifies itself as not a psychotherapy. It doesn't include the ordinary means and methods, nor does it even present itself as for what most psychotherapies are for. What an interesting, and perhaps creative, new idea.

The pathway to creative new ideas is to put yourself in a position of being quite willing to accept the criticism, not as a weapon aimed at destroying what you hold dear, but rather as an interesting and useful springboard to creative new ideas. Let the criticisms come close. Deprive them of their aggressive impact by creative speculation about what creative ideas can present themselves if the criticisms are well and truly taken as true and effective criticisms. Turning criticisms to constructively creative use replaces their aggressive evilness with golden springboards to creative new ideas.

3.4 Use your own criticisms and attacks as challenges to creative new ideas

In your writings, your teachings, your relationships with colleagues, you may have well-honed skills as a professional to be reckoned with, as tough and hard. You can find the problems and the difficulties, the faults, the fatal flaw, the loose thinking, the wrong logic. You can analyze an idea, a program, and take it apart bit by bit. When you criticize something, it is in trouble because your criticisms have teeth, and you are almost always right. When you put your attention on a proposal, an idea, it may as well slink away because it is going to be defeated. You are a fine attacking machine.

The challenge is not to stop being so negative, so critical and attacking. The challenge is to do a fine job of criticizing and attacking, but do not stop there. The challenge is to see whether you have what it takes to take one giant leap into deadly criticisms and attacks, and then to take a second giant leap into the realm of creative new ideas. Do you have the courage and the ability to come up with creative new ideas?

The challenge is to go far beyond (a) showing that you are right, that your criticisms and attacks cannot be dislodged, defeated, dismissed, set aside. The challenge is to go beyond (b) getting your adversary to accept your own approach, your own way of thinking, beyond seeing their own approach in tatters and taking the defeated step of bowing to the superiority of your own approach. 'My gods are unworthy; I accept the superiority of your god.' 'My approach is decimated by your criticisms and your attacks; I humbly accept your better approach.'

The challenge is to go beyond (c) telling the criticized and attacked adversary what it has to do to address the criticisms and the attacks. 'You need more research on this and that. You have to utilize these recent developments. You need a more sophisticated way of dealing with this problem.' The challenge is to go beyond (d) a rational, sensible, non-creative alternative or solution. It is simply not enough to offer an alternative or a solution. This may well offer an alternative or a solution. This may well go beyond being merely critical and attacking. But it falls far short of entering the realm of creative new ideas.

Here is the creative challenge. You may have done a superb job of criticizing and attacking your adversary on the issue of how to do research, on what dreams mean, on the positive mental health movement, on how to treat attention deficit disorder, on the postmodern movement, on psychoanalytic thought, on assessment and evaluation, on the diagnostic system. The creative challenge is to go beyond your criticisms and attacks, and to provide creative new ideas, to offer creative new ideas that shine with the glow of creative new ideas. If your criticisms and attacks have leveled psychoanalytic thought or the diagnostic system, what do you have to offer that shimmers with creativity? That is the creative challenge. Are you able to use your own criticisms and attacks as challenges to creative new ideas?

4. What can account for both the cause and the effect? How can the cause be the effect and the effect be the cause?

In the field of psychotherapy, it is generally taken for granted that there are causes and there are effects. This is built into the common way of thinking, and many of the standard practices are based upon there being causes and effects. Therapists are to identify the causes of patients' problems. If therapists do these things, then here are the supposed effects on the patients. This particular treatment has that supposed effect on this particular mental disorder.

Creative new ideas can come by starting with some identified cause and effect, and being ready to ask two questions. One question is: what can account for both the cause and the effect? Look for something that can underlie both the apparent cause and the apparent effect, and can account for both the cause and the effect. Yes, this cause causes that effect, but here is something deeper, something beneath, something that can explain and can account for both the apparent cause and the apparent effect. In the field of psychotherapy, we know that cause A leads to effect B. It is supported by research. Virtually every approach knows that A is the cause and B is the effect. It is taken for granted as true because it is true. In working with this particular case, I know that B is caused by A, that A leads to B. The client shows B, and all the clinical data point toward B coming from A, because A causes B.

When the question is 'what can account for both A and B?' we are led to finding a creative new idea, namely that C seems to account for both A and B! A doesn't cause B. C causes both of them. What a creative new idea, and it came largely from being able to ask what can account for both the apparent cause and the apparent effect. That is one question.

A second question is: what creative ideas can be brought forth by reversing what is ordinarily thought of as the cause and the effect? Try thinking that what you ordinarily accept as the effect can be the cause of what you ordinarily think of as the cause, and what you ordinarily think of as the cause can be the effect of what you ordinarily think of as the effect. In other words, if you generally hold that Y causes Z, or in this particular instance that Y causes Z, try reversing the sequence so that you can consider that Z causes Y, and see what interesting creative ideas emerge by using this second question.

This second question is simply reversing cause Y and effect Z. This is not quite the same as adopting a position that whatever you hold as a cause can itself be seen as the effect of antecedent causes so that Z is caused by Y, Y is caused by X, X is caused by W, and so on.

Here are a few examples of stirring up some mildly creative ideas by asking: (a) what might be understood as the cause of both the apparent cause and the apparent effect? and (b) what interesting, and perhaps creative, ideas might be stirred up by reversing what is ordinarily accepted as the cause and the effect?

(1) Richard was old, was living in the same small house where he and Kate had lived until she died a few years ago. He had become somewhat quieter lately, did not eat as well as he used to, had some trouble mowing the lawn

and cleaning the house, but he managed. He still liked going to church, reading, and listening to music. His son talked with him about moving to a retirement center, which didn't seem a bad idea because he had been feeling quite lonely in the last months or so, but he was doing all right.

When he became quite upset and gloomy because he forgot to put his garbage out, and he left the iron plugged in all night, his son referred him to a psychotherapist. Dr Bell was a young fellow, but Richard left after a few sessions. The same happened with Dr Lazlo, who prescribed drugs for Richard's mild 'depression'. The bouts of depression became much worse until Richard was referred to Dr Yao, an older female psychiatrist who saw Richard twice a week in psychodynamic therapy.

That was when two interesting things happened. After two or three sessions, the bouts of severe depression lifted. That was interesting, and so too were the abrupt returns of the depressive episodes when Dr Yao guided Richard toward termination of treatment after four months, and then after nearly a year of what proved to be almost three years of psychodynamic therapy.

Now we can ask the first question: what underlying third thing might be seen as causing both the apparent cause and the apparent effect? What might account both for the depression and the seeking of sessions with the psychiatrist? The common idea is that the patient has problems and seeks treatment for the problems. If the patient is depressed, he needs treatment, he seeks treatment, he is referred for treatment. The problem comes first. The problem is the cause, and the treatment is the effect. The first question invites a creative possibility that some third thing can underlie and cause both. What might that third thing be?

Suppose that there was something in Richard that wanted to be with someone who showed genuine interest in him, to have a little friendly closeness like he used to have with his wife, to have someone special in his personal world. When he was a little gloomy, low, depressed, his son was there for him, but not much. A few people in the church group might have provided that for him, but that didn't work out. The first therapist was a young fellow, and that didn't offer Richard much. The second therapist handed him pills, and that didn't do it for Richard.

But Dr Yao was just right. Not only was she an older woman, but she would have sessions with him several times a week, and he reveled in her being so interested in him, in providing friendly closeness. He liked being with her. She was so special for him. The 'depression' went away after a few times of being with Dr Yao, and only returned briefly when she made noises about their no longer being together.

Just as an interesting possibility, could it be that both the 'depression' and the seeking of 'treatment' might be accounted for by something in Richard that wanted to be with someone who showed a little genuine interest in him, who would be with him for an extended period, who could offer a sense of friendly closeness? Could a creative possibility be that both the cause, i.e. the patient's problems, and the effect, i.e. seeking treatment, were caused by something underlying both? At least here is a creative possibility raised by the first question.

The second question is: what creative ideas can be brought forth by simply reversing the apparent cause and the apparent effect? If the commonly held sequence is that first there are problems, and then the patient seeks treatment, if the cause is the problem and the effect is the treatment, then what creative ideas might be put front and center if the order is reversed? What if the seeking of treatment can be thought of as the cause of the problems?

Could it be that Richard would have been able to be with Dr Yao if he said that he was looking for someone who had genuine interest in him, someone offering a little friendly closeness, someone who would offer this for a truly extended period? Perhaps, but probably not. How could he get to be with Dr Yao and to stay with her for such a long time? Perhaps cause and effect might be reversed. Perhaps the depression was the entry ticket to being with Dr Yao. Perhaps the wanting to be with someone like Dr Yao caused the depression. Perhaps a creative case can be made that the 'effect' caused the 'cause', that referral to and treatment by the right person can cause the problems, the difficulties, the mental disorder.

This is one example of at least considering the possibility of bringing forth some creative ideas by asking (a) whether some third thing can cause both the commonly presumed cause and its commonly presumed effect, and (b) whether the commonly presumed cause–effect order can be reversed.

(2) Sarah is having more bouts of drinking and of nasty explosions at Mario, the fellow she lives with. What caused these effects? The apparent cause was Mario's spending time with another woman.

Let us consider the creative possibility that a third something can help account for both the apparent cause and the apparent effect. Sarah's younger sister and brother know that Sarah has an inner experiencing of being unwanted, rejected, alone. Suppose that this painful inner experiencing helps account for her being uncannily skilled in selecting men who will leave her, abandon her, and in doing the right things to get people to leave her feeling unwanted, rejected, alone. Her own inner experiencing of being unwanted, rejected, alone is the underlying cause of both the apparent cause, i.e. Mario's abandoning her, and the apparent effect, i.e. her drinking and nasty explosions.

> *(3) Pavel is from a lower-class family. He marries a woman whose family is wealthy, highly educated, part of the nobility. After they are married, Pavel is treated by his wife's family as an outsider, an unworthy intruder who doesn't really belong in the family. As a result, Pavel feels hurt, rejected, unworthy, unwanted by the family. To Pavel and his confidants, the cause is the family's slights and put-downs, their rejections and their superiority, and the effect is Pavel's feeling of being the unworthy outsider. He should stand up to the nasty family, or strike out on his own, or even consider leaving his wife.*

How can the apparent cause be an effect, and how can the apparent effect be a cause? Suppose that Pavel's feeling of being a lower-class, unwanted outsider is seen as the cause of his being drawn toward the upper-class family, and his marrying his upper-class wife, and his being in situation after situation in which the family look down on him, reject him as an unwanted outsider. In this reversal, his bad feelings are the cause of his inserting himself in the upper-class family, and the slights and rejections of the upper-class family are the effects of the importance of his having feelings of not belonging, of being an unwanted intruder. What was an apparent cause becomes an effect, and what was an apparent effect becomes a cause.

> *(4) Mary was a saint. She took care of her aged and frail parents after their accident, and she was indispensable to them. She dedicated herself to their daily care, and even moved into the family home to be a constant carertaker. As a result, Mary withdrew more and more from having a life of her own, and became increasingly devoted, dedicated, and also increasingly lifeless, grim, numb. A few of her former friends were worried, wanted her to 'get help', to 'see someone', to have a life of her own. They saw her as a drained saint who was showing the effects of dedicating herself to taking care of her parents.*

What was the cause of Mary's becoming increasingly grim, numb, lifeless? It seemed that the cause was her 'excessive' dedication and devotion to taking care of her aged parents. Suppose that we try a creative reversal of apparent cause and effect. Could it be that becoming increasingly grim, numb and lifeless could somehow cause Mary to become increasingly dedicated and devoted to taking care of her old parents? Perhaps it was important for Mary to become quite grim, numb, lifeless. How could she help bring that about? Having more bacon for breakfast wouldn't especially work, nor would wearing some silly new caps or jogging three times a week rather than two. However, a complete and thorough dedication and devotion to taking round-the-clock care of her aged parents might well do the trick. In a twinkle, what had been the cause is now the effect, and what had been the effect is now the cause.

A second way of arriving at a creative new idea is to explore the possibility that some underlying third thing can help account both for the apparent cause, namely Mary's high-powered dedication and devotion to taking care of her aged parents, and for the apparent effect, namely her becoming increasingly lifeless, grim and numb. Picture that the underlying third thing consists of a deeper sense of being thoroughly unappreciated, used, taken advantage of. It was important for Mary to undergo this important deeper experiencing, and it is this important deeper experiencing that helps account for both her exceeding dedication and devotion to her aged parents ('See how they don't appreciate me, use me, take advantage of me?'), and her being so lifeless, grim and numb ('See how they don't appreciate me, use me, take advantage of me?').

It is common to take for granted that here is the cause and here is the effect, and there can be good reasons for being confident about this being the cause of that effect, and that being the effect of this cause. However, you can go further if you start with the cause–effect relationship and want to enter the realm of creative new ideas. Going further into the realm of creativity does not mean that you are taking issue with the cause–effect relationship there in front of you. You are not arguing with this as the cause and that as the effect. However, in order to stir up some interesting creative new ideas, be willing to ask: (a) what might be thought of as a third thing that might help to account for both that cause and that effect? (b) if we reverse cause and effect, how might this cause be seen as an effect, and how might this effect be a cause?

5. Start with the idea that 'we probably got it backwards' or 'if it is generally taken for granted, it is probably wrong'

If you are willing to play the mischievous game of applying both principles, they can carry you into the land of creative new ideas.

5.1 We probably got it backwards

We walked inside the boundaries of this method in section 4 above. Now we can use this method more directly to touch or to be touched by some creative new ideas.

The method begins by searching for some principle or proposition that is taken as true, that is assumed to be true, that is taken for granted, that is the accepted way of thinking in the field of psychotherapy practice or theory or research. Look for something that is essentially unquestioned, something that is part of the basic foundation of the field. Then apply the principle that 'we probably got it backwards', but apply it in the privacy of your home or office because you might be in big trouble if you apply it in the professional public.

Here are a few examples. The game invites you to think of some further examples on your own.

(a) In most sciences, it is generally accepted that if something exists, it can be measured. If we apply our principle, then the field of psychotherapy is inclined to reverse this way of thinking, and to presume that if it can be measured, then it must exist. We probably got it backwards.

Since the field has measures of things like ego strength, schizophrenia, tears in the working alliance, organ inferiorities, actualization drives, conceptual schemata, repressed affects, anomie, self-efficacy, supraordinate cognitions, witches, wandering wombs, elves and gnomes, then it follows that these things must of course exist. We have measures of them.

The field has an unending production capacity of measures, scales and tests for an endless flow of things that are to be measured, and the measures are tested, probed, criterioned and rigored to two decimal places. The field is steeped in a myriad of things that are presumed to be real, true and existing because we have measures of them, and we think this way because we started with a principle that most sciences held dear, and then we probably got it backwards.

You are beginning to inhale creative fumes when you think along these lines: 'So if having a measure can mean that things like schizophrenia or cognitive schemas may not be real, not exist, then ... hmmm ...' You are within breathing range of some creative new ideas.

(b) In many sciences, first you get some understanding of the phenomenon, and then you go looking for its causes. 'It is quite evident, in fact, that one cannot think of investigating anything whatsoever about the causes of phenomena without having studied the phenomena themselves and having acquired some understanding of them' (Duhem, 1996: 27). First get some understanding of the phenomenon, and then search for its causes. A detective or a car mechanic or a physician first takes a reasonably careful look at the phenomenon, and that understanding can be helpful in guiding the search for causes.

In applying the principle that we probably got it backwards, suppose we look for instances where the field of psychotherapy starts with favorite grand causes and then finds phenomena that are to be understood in terms of the favorite grand causes. For example, suppose that one favorite grand cause consists of poor or inadequate or wrong thoughts or cognitions. Then the proponents can find all sorts of phenomena that are to be understood as examples of poor or inadequate or wrong thoughts or cognitions. If we start with the grand cause as inadequate infant–mother relationships, we have a ready-built understanding of the adult feeling of being uneasy by oneself. If the cause lies in inadequate resolution of the grieving process, we can understand phenomena involving the death of a loved one.

How can we enter the realm of creative ideas by applying the principle that we probably got it backwards? Instead of thinking of her sudden bouts of sobbing as the effects of an inadequate grieving process, study her bouts of crying on their own, afresh, something to try to understand, quite apart from some inadequate grieving process. Set aside the inadequate grieving process, and try to see where she is when she sobs, the exact circumstances of the sobbing, what she is thinking and what she is feeling when she is sobbing, what she thinks and feels about the sobbing, what happens after the sobbing. The creative ideas can come when you set aside the event as an effect of this or that cause, and instead try to understand the event on its own, and then seek the causes.

In the field of psychotherapy it is quite common to start with a cause and to understand that phenomenon as some sort of effect of that predetermined cause. Accordingly, the grand cause is the 'diagnosis', and the phenomenon is pre-understood and pre-categorized as a 'symptom' of that diagnosis. That fellow hears a voice inside his head, and the voice is pre-determined to be a symptom of psychosis, with 'psychosis' as the cause that allows the voice to be thought of as a symptom of the psychosis. However, suppose we apply the principle that we probably got it backwards, and let go of understanding the voice as a symptom of psychosis or anything else. Suppose that we try to understand this fellow's voice on its own. What is the phenomenon in question? Is it when he heard the voice in his head, or when he or someone else had worries and misgivings about a person hearing voices inside his head? In either case, what were the exact circumstances? Precisely what was the voice saying? How was the voice saying it? What was the person thinking and feeling when he heard the voice?

In some fairly common ways, the field of psychotherapy starts with pre-determined sets of causes, and the causes lend a pre-determined set of understandings to many phenomena. Creative juices can be put into motion when you start with the phenomenon, poke inside and around the phenomenon to gain further and deeper understanding, and then move on to the search for causes.

(c) In many fields, it is accepted that first you assemble observations, facts, data, and then you follow careful procedures to arrive at a general principle. Suppose that we apply the idea that in the field of psychotherapy we probably got it backwards. See how applying this idea can foster some creative thinking if we suggest that the field of psychotherapy starts with an accepted general principle and then assembles observations, facts and data that come from, are generated by, are inclined to be limited and restricted to, and therefore tend to provide support for, the initial general principle.

You can enter the land of creative possibilities by starting with some generally accepted dictum or truth, whether it refers to practice or theory or research, and then being ready and willing to see what creative possibilities can appear when you apply the principle that we probably got it backwards. There is another way.

5.2 If it is generally taken for granted, it is probably wrong

It is generally taken for granted that if it is generally taken for granted, it is probably closer to the truth. If there are ten judges who are judging an event, you can usually feel more confidence if all ten judges agree with one another. What is called 'consensual validation' expresses this exceedingly common way of thinking. If most of the field takes for granted some principle, idea, proposition, it gains added strength and moves closer to being a canon, a law, a truth, a dictum. It can be a powerful persuader to say that something is generally taken for granted in the field.

The doorway into the land of creative possibilities is the somewhat wicked notion that if it is indeed taken for granted, then it is probably wrong. If it is a solid part of what is accepted by the mainstream, by tradition, by the field, by practitioners or researchers or theoreticians, then it is probably wrong.

This principle can be considered somewhat wicked because you don't have to really believe that if it is generally taken for granted it is probably wrong. This principle does not have to be true. Instead, this wicked principle happens to be quite useful in merely opening up creative possibilities. It can be quite useful to play with the idea that if it is generally taken for granted then it is probably wrong. You don't have to believe this idea, just use it to enter the world of creative ideas.

When you find something that is generally taken for granted, adopting the notion that it is probably wrong does not tell you what the creative possibility is, or even point you in the right direction. It merely says that you can let go of whatever is taken for granted. The creative possibilities are not located right here. Look elsewhere, but where to look is up to you.

Looking for creative possibilities is usually helped when you pass by plausible alternatives to whatever is generally taken for granted. For most 'truths' that are taken for granted, there are a few plausible alternatives that are not especially popular or fashionable, although a small contingency may cherish the plausible alternative. Pass by these plausible alternatives, and pass by benign and sensible modifications to whatever is generally taken for granted. These benign modifications may be appealing, may seem sound and sensible, but they are not especially the doorways into the land of creative possibilities. Instead of looking for plausible alternatives or benign modifications, start with what is generally taken for granted and let yourself boldly sail here and there in the land of creative possibilities. Range far and wide. Go to new and exciting places.

Here are some examples of using this principle to start from what is generally taken for granted and then to launch into a creative voyage.

Start with the somewhat common idea that concepts from different conceptual systems can be combined to yield a better conceptual system. If this concept gets at a part of the truth, and that concept gets at another part of the truth, then combining them can get you even closer to the truth. Here is a plank in the integrative way of building better conceptual systems. It may well be a relatively common idea, one that is generally taken for granted. It may even be that you yourself take this common principle for granted.

You are putting on your creative hat when you can proclaim, 'If it is generally taken for granted, it is probably wrong!' Go ahead. Follow it up. If that generally-taken-for-granted idea is wrong, then how can that lead you toward some creative new ideas? Here are a few attempts to start there and to arrive at some creative new ideas:

(a) The way that is commonly accepted suggests that some phenomenon or event is thought of as made up of the sum of its parts. For example, a headache may be thought of as made up of so many parts that are neurophysiological plus so many parts that are psychological. On the basis of this common way of looking at things, if a neurophysiological examination finds little or no neurophysiological explanation or cause, it can be sensible to refer the patient to psychology with the understanding that there probably is a psychological explanation or cause.

This may be interesting, but the creative idea can be ushered in when your way of thinking shifts to a creative idea that something, e.g. a headache, can be open to a full explanation and description neurophysiologically, and psychologically, and from other relevant viewpoints. If the headache is not explainable and describable neurophysiologically, it may also not be explainable and describable psychologically. Instead of the explanations and descriptions adding up to 100 per cent, each mode of explanation and description can vary from 1 to 99 per cent, essentially independently of one another. The headache may be quite understandable neurologically, and also quite understandable physiologically, and quite understandable sociologically, and quite understandable psychoanalytically, and quite understandable in terms of learning theory, and quite understandable in experiential terms, cognitive terms, Gestalt terms, and so on. These creative possibilities may not pay off, but they can be found by adopting the principle that if it is taken for granted, it is probably wrong.

(b) If we continue from the generally accepted idea that concepts from different conceptual systems can be combined to yield a better overall conceptual system, suppose that you run into occasions when this generally accepted idea is a conspicuous failure. For example, if you are trying to improve on your prediction of a series of throws of a die, the effectiveness of your mathematical concepts may not be increased, and may even be conspicuously decreased, if you try to combine your mathematical concepts with concepts of libidinal energy or the law of effect or the concept of cognitive permeability.

At this point, you can easily conclude that there are obvious conditions under which trying to combine concepts from different conceptual systems doesn't work. Or you can enter the realm of creativity by trying to clarify the conditions under which it can be fruitful or relatively fruitless to try to combine concepts from different conceptual systems.

(c) Suppose that you hold to the concept of 'unconscious impulses', and you are considering combining it with the concept of 'growth force' from another conceptual system. You can try to combine the two while preserving the characteristics of your concept of unconscious impulses, or you can enter the realm of creativity by, for example, allowing the combination to make for significant modifications in each. Perhaps, for example, the intrusive concept of a benign growth force can blend with unconscious impulses by allowing for bad, unpleasant unconscious impulses and also good, pleasant unconscious impulses. This is a significant departure from the traditionally bad, problematic, nasty impulses that are taken for granted as making up the unconscious.

These are three forays into the realm of the creative, all beginning from the taken-for-granted idea that concepts from different conceptual systems can be combined to yield a better conceptual system, and fueled by the creative principle that if it is generally taken for granted it is probably wrong.

You can start with almost any idea that is generally taken for granted, consider that the taken-for-granted idea is probably wrong, and then look for the creative possibilities. In opening the door to bold creative ideas, do not stop at essentially retaining the taken-for-granted idea and adding a conditional clause or a slight modification here and there. Instead, creative possibilities ask that you let go of the whole taken-for-granted idea as all wrong.

Here are a few examples. Try to let go of these taken-for-granted ideas, without quibbling or not really letting them go, and see for yourself what creative possibilities you can come up with if you keep repeating, 'This is generally taken for granted so it is probably wrong!' (a) Psychotherapy is to treat, reduce, help get rid of, mental illnesses and disorders, symptoms, presenting complaints and psychological problems. (b) People generally seek pleasure and avoid pain. (c) Most psychotherapies work because of the therapist's methods and interventions, and the therapist–client relationship. Can you generate some creative possibilities by using the principle that if it is generally taken for granted, it is probably wrong?

This chapter suggests some ways to start from an idea with some possibilities of becoming a creative idea and then to develop this idea into a full-fledged creative idea. We now turn to another way of coming up with creative ideas.

CHAPTER 7

Instead of Being the One Who Creates, Be the One Who is Created

It may be common for you to put yourself in the position of being the creator, the one who comes up with creative ideas. The creative idea comes to you, and you develop it, you use it, you apply it. You do creative things to whatever you work on. You apply creative ideas to your subject matter. You are the one who creates. You may even learn new and better ways of coming up with creative ideas and of applying them in new and better ways.

In this picture, you play one role, and the created idea plays another role. Your role is to create the creative idea, to build it, to produce it. You are the creator, and it is the created. The forces of change lie in you and act upon the creative idea. Your role is that of the active one, and the creative idea is the passive fruit of your creation. You act upon it, and it is acted upon. When the act of creation is completed, something new is created out there. Your role is that of the creator, and its role is to be what is created by you.

Picture that the roles are reversed. Instead of your doing creativity unto others, you let creativity do itself unto you. Picture that you submit yourself to what creativity can do to you. You are the object of creative forces. Creative forces can act upon you, can change you, can exert themselves upon you. Picture that you willingly submit yourself to the forces of creativity, even to the point that creative forces bring about changes in you, can radically alter you, can transform you. Picture that you remove virtually all restrictions so that creative forces can take you through wholesale and complete personal transformation. Instead of being the creator, you are the created.

How can you allow creative forces to act upon you? One way is to allow an experiential session to guide you through an experiential session. Picture that you are going through an experiential session with a teacher-guide, an experiential therapist. Or picture that you are sufficiently skilled to go through an experiential session by yourself. Even further, picture that you have willingly committed yourself to a lifetime of experiential sessions.

Each experiential session is a fresh opportunity to actively engage powerful creative forces that can act upon you, that can take you through basic, fundamental, deep-seated, core personal changes, that can release qualitative changes in you, that can utterly transform you. This is one way of submitting yourself to what powerful creative forces can do to you.

My consistent and strong impression is that psychotherapists are notoriously reluctant to submit themselves to whatever creative forces might do to them, that psychotherapists are characteristically among the least enthusiastic in throwing themselves into the path of creative forces. If the invitation were extended to various groups such as psychotherapists, high school teachers, truck drivers, athletes, cooks and healthcare workers, my impression is that psychotherapists would rank among the lowest in terms of acceptance of the invitation. If the invitation were extended to people in general, my impression is that, of the decliners, an impressively high proportion would be likely to be psychotherapists.

For psychotherapists, my impression is that allowing oneself to be a client can be quite tolerable, especially if the therapeutic forces do not especially include anything that can threaten serious, deep-seated change in the inner core of who and what the person is. In general, it is as if psychotherapists don't typically offer serious, deep-seated change in the inner core of their clients, and are powerfully reluctant to voluntarily submit themselves to such serious change, whether this means putting themselves in the role of clients who might undergo such deep-seated personal change or, even more unthinkably, undergoing such deep-seated change in their own self-change sessions by and for themselves (Mahrer, 2002b).

Would you be ready and willing to let creative forces act upon you? To the extent that creative forces are thought of as benign and good, you may be inclined to say yes, especially if you have some generally nondescript but friendly picture of what takes place if you agree to be the object of creative forces. On the other hand, your generally welcoming state may shift a bit if you are taken to a small room with only the large wooden chair; you are sitting in the chair; your feet, legs, hands, arms, back and head are strapped in; you are blindfolded; and you are told that, when you press the lever under your left index finger, the creative forces will act upon you with full force.

When you were in the role of creator, you rarely if ever considered the reactions of whatever was the object of your creativity. Now that you are in the role of the object of creative forces, the circumstances can become somewhat ominous, and you can find yourself raising some serious issues:

(a) Before it gets started, just how far can the creative forces go? I can accept some surface changes, or changes that I would like, but might the changes be in important parts of my world, things I may not want changed? What about changes in me? I don't think I want deep-seated changes in me, not drastic changes, not basic changes. That won't happen, right? The answer is: 'You can push the lever or you can not. That is all.'

(b) I can accept or decline the change, right? If I don't like what it does to me, it won't happen, right? I have veto power, right? The answer is: 'You can push the lever or you can not. That is all.'

(c) It starts when I push down on this lever, right? So where is the stop lever? If I lift my finger, then everything stops, right? If I want to stop, I can stop it, right? I don't think I want to hear the answer. The answer is: 'You can push the lever or you can not. That is all.'

I don't know of any such room that has harnessed the creative forces and can direct them onto you. I don't know of any generally accepted way that you can let creative forces act upon you, even if you say that you are ready and willing to try. I don't know of any contraption or pill or program that has a generally accepted track record of bathing you in creativity, of concentrating creative forces on you, even if you are a ready and willing object.

Even if you are genuinely ready and willing to be the object of creative forces, the burden is not necessarily on someone else to produce the room with the chair, to offer the contraption or the pill or the program, to provide you with sufficient evidence that this puts you in the position of being the object of creative forces. In this scenario, you put yourself in the role of the judge who judges whether what someone else offers is adequate or inadequate as far as you are concerned. In this scenario, the burden is on the other person, not on you.

There is another scenario, a different scenario in which the burden lies mainly on you, rather than on some other person. You are the one who searches for and perhaps finds a way to make yourself the object of creative forces. You are the one who may be excited and scared by what can happen if you do this, if you allow these creative forces to act upon you, to do things to you, to affect you, to bathe you in the forces of creative change. You are the one who knows that doing this can substantially change your ideas, can creatively change the way you think and what you think, can allow creative forces to alter what is truly deeper in you, can transform you into something you may not know or control or expect. You are the one who finds this way of being the object of creative forces, of being the one who is created, who is ready and willing for what can be created in and of you.

You may be the one who finds a faraway place, who spends six months living the life of an altogether different person who (a) joins with others in creating, producing, building, exploring, discovering, developing altogether new things, worlds, ideas; (b) joins with others in deep daily meditation in your journey toward a state of enlightenment and liberation; (c) joins with others in having daily sessions of inviting powerful forces to create the qualitatively new person you can become, and daily sessions of learning optimal ways of being and behaving.

These are merely some examples of what you may do if you are searching for ways of submitting yourself to creative forces, of being the object of creative forces that can act upon you. You are the one who must look for a way or ways that you follow for yourself. You are probably not used to being the object of creative forces that act upon you, that do things to you, that have impacts and effects upon you. So why put yourself in such a position? Why even enter the room? Why sit in the chair? Why press the lever to let the creative forces act upon you?

One answer is that being the object of creative forces, being the one who is created, putting yourself in the hands of creative forces, undergoing what creative forces can do to you, can enhance your own creativity, your own ability to come up with creative ideas. There are at least three ways this can happen, and each brings some serious risks.

1. Receiving, welcoming, embracing what creative forces can do to you can make you more able to be receiving, welcoming, embracing creative new ideas

The extreme form means that you put yourself in a state of wholly receiving, welcoming, embracing creative forces that can utterly transform you into a wholesale new person. Both parts are extreme.

You wholly open up to the creative forces. You give yourself wholly to the creative forces. Instead of closing your eyes, gritting your teeth and steeling yourself to what the creative forces can do to you, you open your eyes, open your arms and run into the creative forces. You actively receive the creative forces. You actively welcome them. You actively embrace them. You throw yourself into the abyss. You actively hurl yourself into the fire of creativity. You actively expose yourself to whatever creativity can do to you.

You follow the path of exploring deep inside your inner region and discovering parts that you never knew existed. Entering down into the other deeper world calls for the boldest of measures. Discovering what lurks in the inner deeper world calls for the courage of utterly fearless discovery. And there is more.

You wholly receive, welcome and embrace what the creative forces you discovered can do to you. Let them end your very existence and bring into fresh existence a whole new you. Let them utterly transform you into being a whole new person that you can become. Let the deeper parts that you discovered become integral parts of the person you can become by allowing those discovered parts to become integral parts of a transformed, whole new you. The net result of your becoming more receiving, welcoming and embracing of creative forces is that you are becoming much more receiving, welcoming and embracing of creative ideas. They can find you. You like them. They gravitate toward you. You see them where other people cannot and do not see them. Creative ideas come to you because you are much more receptive, welcoming and embracing of creative new ideas. By actively opening yourself up to the extreme of what creative forces can do to you, namely to create a radical, transformed, whole new you, you are actively opening yourself up to receiving, welcoming and embracing creative new ideas.

Submitting yourself to wholesale personal transformation can involve entering into the inner deeper world, into the world of the great unknown. You leave go of what you know, and you walk around in the dark. You can meet things that are utterly strange and alien, far beyond the world of the familiar.

Being seasoned and skilled in entering the inner world of the unknown can make it easier for you to enter the world of creative ideas. You can be welcoming toward ideas that are strange, unknown, unfamiliar. Instead of being ready to find parts of an other you, parts that can surely transform you into a qualitatively new person, you can be ready to enter the world of creative ideas with perhaps powerful implications for the world in which you live.

Personal transformation can mean wholly submitting yourself to what inner creative forces can do to you, letting these inner creative forces transform you into a qualitatively whole new person. You can actually welcome submitting yourself to the possibilities that are deep inside you.

In much the same way, going through your own personal transformation can make you more welcoming and able to submit to creative ideas. You can allow them to play onto you, affect you, change the ideas you have, take hold of you, work their magic on you.

When you can welcome creative forces into actually transforming you, you can thereby be much more receptive to creative new ideas.

2. You can become free of hindrances to creative new ideas

If you allow creative forces to transform you into a qualitatively new person, one of the delightful consequences can be that you become a new person who is largely free of the former hindrances, resistances, obstacles, blocks to creative new ideas. Whatever they were, they can be essentially gone, or at least substantially reduced.

You had been a person who embraced the cognitive behavioral approach, knew the names of some other approaches, but had never had a beer with them, talked seriously with them, visited their homes. Now you are different. You still embrace the cognitive behavioral approach, but you have read some articles by proponents of other approaches, you have attended symposia of other approaches, and you actually have friends from other approaches, friends with whom you talk and to whom you listen, on topics of mutual interest. You have indeed changed.

You had been exceedingly vigilant and on guard against new ideas. They were not 'creative,' they were dangerous, threatening. They were an enemy menace. You had attacked them, refused to listen to them, put up barriers against them, kept them at a safe distance. Now you are different. You still won't see them as creative new ideas, but you can at least accept that they exist, and you can admit that they threaten you. You have undergone a massive change.

What you had believed you had believed absolutely. There was not a whisper of doubt. Your fundamental beliefs were rock-solid certainties, wholly unquestioned, thoroughly accepted, eternal truths, wholly unassailable. When you allowed yourself to undergo wholesale change, the consequence was that something was conspicuously missing, and a new quality took its place. What was missing was the rock-solid certainty, the unassailable truth of what you wholly accepted as true. What took its place was a seemingly new part that could acknowledge that you had no room for doubt or for challenges to what you believed, that you believed wholeheartedly in what you believed. This new part could say with wise humor, 'Don't even bother questioning my beliefs, because my faith is unquestioned. So there!'

However, there is always a risk. Creative forces can transform you into a whole new person, but the person you become may well have the same, or even greater, hindrances to creative new ideas. Nor can you make deals or place conditions on the kind of person you become if you submit yourself to what creative forces can do to you. Transformation cannot proceed if you make a precondition: 'I will agree to submit myself for transformation if I can become a person who is essentially free of my hindrances to creative new ideas.'

3. You may become a wellspring of creative new ideas

The possibility, for better or for worse, is that submitting yourself to creative forces can transform you into being a veritable wellspring of creative new ideas, and this seems to have little or nothing to do with your history of producing creative new ideas. If you have a track record of producing creative new ideas, you can become far more of a virtuoso. If you occasionally came up with some creative new ideas, you can be transformed into a major resource of creative new ideas. Even if your history seems consistently free of creative new ideas, with essentially no little creative hintings from childhood on, you nevertheless could become a wholesale producer of creative new ideas. Your track record plays little or no role in the powerful effects of submitting yourself to what creative forces can do to you.

The person who you are may crave having creative new ideas, may want to be a wellspring of creative new ideas. One way to achieve these sought-after goals is to let go of your craving, your wanting, your hoping. Simply give them up altogether, and instead passively submit yourself to becoming the whole new person you are capable of becoming. Undergo wholesale transformation, and one possibility is that you will emerge as a wellspring of creative new ideas.

However, once again, the magic potion works only if there are no preconditions. You may become a wellspring of creative new ideas. You may not. You risk becoming transformed into a very fine candy bar or bus driver or good friend, but without being a wellspring of creative new ideas. In any case, the choice is yours. Are you ready and willing to allow creative forces to transform you into whatever you can become?

Creative new ideas are best friends with change. They go with change. They imply change. They produce change. Where there are creative new ideas, there can be change, there almost certainly will be change, change fills the air.

You can enter into the world of creative new ideas by welcoming and embracing your own personal change, rather than disdaining your own personal change, brushing away your own personal change, or producing all sorts of excuses for not welcoming and embracing your own personal change.

This chapter offers three guidelines for letting creative forces bring about changes in you. If you are truly interested in creative new ideas, consider following these three guidelines.

CHAPTER 8

Enter into a 'Creative Relationship' with what You are Studying

Whether you are being a practitioner, a teacher, a supervisor, a theoretician or a researcher, you are almost always in some kind of relationship with whatever you are working on, inquiring into, examining, studying. You almost always have some kind of relationship with the class you are teaching, the student whose thesis you are supervising, the client or patient you are treating, the data you are trying to make sense of, the article you are reading the trainee whom you are supervising, the colleague you are working with, the research subject you are examining, whatever it is that you are studying.

You may have a fairly standard or common relationship with what you are working on, what you are studying, whether the object of your study is the person who is sobbing about her deceased mother, or the plate of magical spaghetti in the dream, or the doctoral student who is so pleased with what happened in the recent session with his client. Or your relationship may be somewhat uncommon, different, out of the mainstream.

In almost any case, it is unlikely that the main purpose of the way you relate is to provide the right conditions for creative new ideas. You probably relate to the other person in ways that seem helpful to get the job done, to do a good job of supervision, of psychotherapy, of understanding whatever you are studying. There can be plenty of ways to relate to whatever you are intent on studying, but few if any of those ways were developed primarily to help you to come up with creative new ideas, to establish what might be called a 'creative relationship' with whatever you are studying.

The purpose of this chapter is (a) to introduce what may be called a 'creative relationship' with what you are studying, (b) to suggest that a promising avenue toward coming up with creative ideas is to have such a creative relationship with what you are studying, and (c) to describe some guidelines for establishing and using a creative relationship with what you are studying.

These guidelines are cast within the field of psychotherapy practice, even though these kinds of relationships seem to be quite rare in psychotherapy practice. The theme is that you can set the stage for creative new ideas by using these guidelines to be in a creative relationship with what you are studying.

1. Both you and what you are studying are to get into a state of heightened feeling

In some other fields, a creative relationship can be one in which you and the thing you are studying both enter in an extraordinary state. For example, you both get into a chamber that spins around with increasing velocity. You are both in a state of significantly reduced or heightened gravity, temperature, pressure.

Picture that you and the client enter into a state of heightened feeling by spending two to five minutes taking rapid deep breaths and exhaling explosively, screaming and yelling as loud as you can, shrieking, bellowing, falling into gales of laughter, throwing your body from side to side, kicking, hitting, flailing.

Suppose that you keep on until there are sensations in and over your body, sensations that are beyond the usual sensations and that seem to take on a life of their own, sensations such as a pleasant dizziness, quivering of muscles in the legs or mouth, an all-over tingling, ripplings of cold or warmth, cascades of shivers or electrical tinglings. Suppose the sensations keep on until you no longer have that abiding sense of awareness, that sense of I-ness or self, that flow of inner private thoughts and inferences

This is an unusual and dramatic way of getting into an exceedingly powerful state of heightened feeling. It may have taken two to four minutes or so. Now picture that both you and the client spend the rest of the session in a state of heightened feeling that is (a) less powerful and extreme than this opening exercise, but (b) more intense than the normal or ordinary state of feeling for both of you in your common ways of being with people in your lives.

Throughout the rest of the session, your voices are deliberately and substantially loud, pumped-up with whatever feeling is present in each or you. It may be that whatever feeling each of you is having is heightened, or it may be that some other feeling is present and heightened. Your speech is rapid, less grammatically correct. Each of you may repeat words and phrases. There are virtually none of the ordinary silences or speaking turns. People who ordinarily are familiar with each of you might not be able to recognize you if they heard audiotapes of you having such heightened feeling.

You have entered into a creative relationship with what you are studying or working with by getting into and remaining in this state of heightened feeling. Here are two ways in which this relationship can be said to be creative:

(a) Quite often, what you may have expected to intensify, to worsen or become more bothersome, does not do so. This can be surprising and can confront you with creative possibilities. For example, the gloomy, depressed, heavy, withdrawn feeling state often does not become even more gloomy and depressed. The ordinary state of feeling tense and anxious does not become more so. An initial state of feeling irritated, annoyed and angry does not worsen and intensify. Even a state of feeling out of touch with reality, of feeling weird and bizarre, of being crazy and psychotic fails to intensify or worsen. How very interesting! You can be face to face with interesting creative possibilities.

Suppose that the person is frightened of falling apart, of truly losing one's mind, of giving up the last vestiges of control, and sinking into the abyss of utter madness. Now suppose that both you and the person hold hands and leap off the ledge, down into the black abyss, shrieking with the absolute terror of what you both know is waiting for both of you. But it doesn't! Miraculously, the dreaded certainty does not happen. Not only can this be magnificently surprising, but it can also be bewilderingly challenging and inviting you to make sense of what did not happen. Creative possibilities are swirling all around you.

(b) When both of you are in the state of heightened feeling, some things can disappear and some other things can appear. Whether the heightened feeling is pleasant or unpleasant, new and uncharacteristic or a heightening of the ordinary state the person was in, some things seem to fade out of existence. The state of gripping anxiety can be gone. The saturnine and gloomy depression is nowhere to be found. What had been so very worrisome and bothersome has moved from center stage. In a symmetrical way, in the state of heightened feeling, some new things seem to appear. Those can be altogether new qualities and characteristics. There can be new feelings. Other parts of the person take center stage.

When both of you have entered into the continuing state of heightened feeling, this new kind of relationship can face you with creative possibilities. Does the very existence of many things seem to be tied to a particular range of feelings? Will a block of ice disappear if the temperature goes above a particular point? Does the nature, content and range of what an observer or researcher or therapist can know about the subject or other person depend upon their sharing a similar state of heightened feeling? When you and the thing you are studying are both in a state of heightened feeling, you can be in a creative relationship, full of creative possibilities.

When the premium is on creative possibilities, you may be willing to see what it can be like for you and the other person, or whatever you are studying, to enter into a state of considerably heightened feeling. Once you both are in this rather unusual state, once the two of you can share this creative relationship, take a creative look. Do some interesting things tend to disappear, go away, change in some impressive way? Do some interesting new things seem to appear, to come about? By entering into this state of heightened feeling, you have helped to establish a creative relationship in which you can touch or be touched by some creative new ideas.

2. You are the teacher-guide, and the other person is the practitioner or researcher

When you are the practitioner, you typically put yourself into the role of the therapist, you treat something about the client, you develop and use the therapist–client relationship, you have a menu of interventions which you apply to your work with the client, you do therapeutic things to your client.

In addition, you tend to put the other person in the complementary role of the client. You are the therapist, and the other person is the client. You are the service provider, and the other person is the service receiver. You are the helper, and the other person is the helpee. You apply the treatment, and the other person receives the treatment. You apply the interventions, and the other person is the object of the interventions.

When you are the researcher, a large part of your role can be doing research things to the subjects, applying the design and methodology to the research subjects, putting the subjects into the experimental or the control conditions, observing and studying your research subjects. Accordingly, the other person is typically in the role of the one who is assessed, studied, observed, tested, put into this or that research condition, cast in the role of

160

the one who is the object of your observation, study, examination, inquiry, research.

The way you relate to the other person, the roles that you are typically in and you nudge the other person to typically fulfill, are largely because those roles help to get the job done. You have a job to do, as the therapist or as the researcher, and the relatively common role of practitioner or of researcher is helpful in your doing your job as practitioner or as researcher.

When you are being the practitioner or the researcher, your main job is not to come up with creative new ideas. Nor is your main job to establish the elegant conditions or context for coming up with creative new ideas. Accordingly, the main emphasis is not especially on establishing a creative relationship with the other person. Even more explicitly, when you are being the practitioner or the researcher, you are probably not dedicated to fulfilling the role of teacher-guide nor the other person to fulfilling the role of the practitioner or of the researcher.

2.1 To open up creative new ideas, consider having a 'creative relationship' with the other person

What is a 'creative relationship'? Instead of your being the therapist or the researcher, you are a 'teacher-guide' who shows the other person what to do, how and why to do it. Instead of the other person being the client, the other person is the practitioner who carries out what is to be carried out in the therapy, who carries out the methods and the procedures that help bring about the aims and goals of the session. Instead of the other person being the research subject, the other person is both the researcher and the subject, both the one who carries out what is to be studied and the one who gathers the observations. In a creative relationship, you are mainly the teacher-guide of the other person, and the other person is mainly the practitioner or the researcher.

Picture a teacher-guide working with another person either for purposes of practice or for purposes of research, study, inquiry. The idea of two people working on the third thing may not be especially common in ordinary psychotherapy or research, but it can be a relationship of choice when it comes to coming up with creative new ideas. Picture a driving instructor showing a student how to drive a car, or the scientist on earth giving instructions to the researcher on the moon about how to scoop up material below the moon's surface. Picture a boxing trainer showing a young boxer how to throw a left hook or a researcher being the teacher-guide who is showing the brilliant colleague how to draw further implications from her brilliant findings. Picture the surgeon showing the surgical resident how to remove the tumor from the brain, or showing the research surgeon how to compare the lung tissue in the four patients whose cancer inexplicably disappeared instead of killing them.

In the creative relationship, you are in the role of teacher-guide, rather than some variation of the ordinary role of practitioner or researcher, and the other person is in the role of the practitioner or researcher, rather than some variation of the ordinary role of client or research subject. The main reason for this creative relationship, the main purpose or aim, is to help create the right context for coming up with creative new ideas, rather than to do psychotherapy or to do research. The main reason or purpose or aim is not to replace the ordinary roles or relationships between therapist and client or researcher and research subject, but to establish the creative relationship to help open up creative new ideas.

2.2 What can be some creative possibilities when you are the teacher-guide and the other person is the practitioner or researcher?

In the ordinary role, you are the psychotherapist, the practitioner, and the other person is the client or patient. In the creative relationship, you are a teacher-guide, and the other person is the practitioner. Your job is to show the other person what to do and how to do it, in the person's carrying out the methods of proceeding through a session.

Here are some gentle hints toward creative possibilities when you are mainly the teacher-guide and the other person is mainly the practitioner, in proceeding through a session of psychotherapy (Mahrer, 1996/2004, 2001c, 2002a):

(a) As the teacher-guide, the therapist leaves so much up to the other person's readiness and willingness. Over and over again, the teacher-guide sees whether the person is ready and willing to do the next step, each little sub-step. The teacher-guide keeps checking: 'Is this OK? Ready to do this? Are you clear?'

One of the creative possibilities arises from the fact that it becomes so conspicuous that much of what most therapists do, most of the time, is to push the clients, to pressure clients, to get clients to be this way or that way. Therapy seems to be revealed as a naked way of therapists pushing clients, of therapists trying to get clients to do this or that. Think this way. Have this way of looking at things. Have these values. Treat your son this way. Be that way with your husband. Don't think that way. Respect this. Don't be that way. Do this. Stop doing that. Be more this way.

The therapist's being in the role of mere teacher-guide not only leaves the other person in the much more powerful role of the practitioner, the one who carries out the methods, but also exposes that so much of what so many therapists do is to push, push, push the client into being the way the therapist wants and doing what the therapist is trying to get the client to do.

When the teacher-guide counts so much on the other person's immediate readiness, the other person can go ahead and do it, or pause for a while, or change it a little this way or that way, or even decline doing it at all. The surprisingly creative possibility is that what is ordinarily called 'resistance' or 'lack of motivation' disappears, mainly because there is little or nothing to resist. The therapist asks, 'Are you ready to do this right now?' The other person says, 'No.' The therapist as teacher-guide almost always says in effect, 'OK.' What is ordinarily called resistance tends to call for something to be resisted, something the therapist is trying to get the patient to see, do, carry out. When the teacher-guide asks whether the person is ready, the other person can be surprisingly free to say yes or no, and either option is just fine. So-called resistance is inclined to extinguish, mainly because the conditions for resistance are no longer present.

When the therapist is simply the teacher-guide, and readiness and willingness are in the hands of the other person, something paradoxical often happens, something strange, something that seems to ask for creative explanation. The other person seems to be surprisingly ready and willing. The person openly takes giant steps into alien territory. The person will do what the person would not ordinarily do in ordinary relationships between therapists and clients. This can make for big in-session changes when the other person has essentially all the mandate, all the right and authority to go ahead or not to, to take the next baby step or not to. It is as if the person is free to do things that the person would not ordinarily do with therapists who have ordinary, non-creative relationships with clients. And something similar seems to be in store for the therapist as teacher-guide.

When the therapist enters into being the teacher-guide and leaves behind the typical role of psychotherapist, it is as if the teacher-guide is freed of so much baggage, is lightened and liberated from so much that the therapist conforms to, abides by, tries to accomplish, almost without knowing that the therapist is functioning within all these heavy restrictions and with all these burdens. The other side of this freedom is the freedom to take some risks, to enter into relatively unknown territory, to do things that therapists do not ordinarily do, to achieve what ordinary therapists do not achieve.

These are some of the creative possibilities when the therapist becomes the teacher-guide and hands the mandate over to the other person's sense of readiness and willingness to carry forward or not.

(b) There can be a substantially new relationship when the person is attending mainly to some attentional center, when the teacher is likewise attending mainly to what the person is attending to, and when neither is attending mainly to the other. Most psychotherapists and clients spend most of the session attending to and talking to one another. In some contrast, something quite different can be happening when the student tracker and the teacher are both attending to the animal tracks in the snow, when the new driver and the driving instructor are both attending to the oncoming trucks in the other lane, when the resident surgeon and the teacher are both attending to the resident's use of the scalpel on the tissues around the heart.

Creative new possibilities can happen when the teacher or guide and the other person are both attending mainly to what the other person is mainly attending to. This creative new relationship can make a difference in how they are with one another and in what can happen as they both attend to and relate to that third thing out there.

(c) You both sacrifice the feelings that go with the roles of therapist and client who attend mainly to one another. When the therapist and the client attend mainly to one another, something special tends to happen, almost aside from the school of therapy or whatever is the focus or goal of the therapy. The 'something special' is that the therapist and the client can, if they create the right kinds of roles for one another, have some special kinds of feelings in being with one another. Sometimes these feelings can be important and pleasurable. Sometimes these feelings can be important and painful.

In any case, when therapist and client are in this creative new relationship, when they are not in the common roles of therapist and client, attending mainly to one another, then many of these important and special feelings are inclined to wash away, to be absent. Here are a few such examples:

(1) The therapist is the client's best friend, the one you can trust, the one you can confide in and tell everything to. The client is the loner who needs a best friend, a trusted confidante.

(2) The therapist is the one who is on your side, is here to defend you. The client is embattled, attacked by others, needs a strong defender.

(3) The therapist is the exemplar of mental health, the ideal one, the optimal one. The client looks for a hero, someone to look up to, to be like.

(4) The therapist is the rock, the grounded, reality-based, solid one. The client is mixed up, at loose ends, needs solid ground, a Rock of Gibraltar.

(5) The therapist is the grand rescuer, the savior, the one who renders the client normal again. The client is shattered, broken, fallen apart.

These are only a few of the many roles and in-session feelings that therapists and clients are inclined to have, for better or for worse, when they spend most of their time attending to and talking to one another. These roles and in-session feelings tend to wash away when the therapist is mainly teacher and the other person is mainly 'practitioner' in the creative new relationship. Try out this creative new relationship between the two people. See what creative new ideas come to you.

(d) There can be some creative possibilities for the actual, in-session, working methods that get things done, which help achieve what psychotherapy is to achieve. If the therapist becomes the teacher-guide, and if the client becomes the practitioner, the one to carry out the methods, then it is likely that some common methods will fade away. For example, the role of what is ordinarily called 'interpretation' would almost certainly come close to non-existence. So too would the method of 'empathy' be inclined to approach extinction when methods are carried out mainly by the person, the practitioner.

It can be interesting to see which relatively common methods can be carried out by the client, the other person, the practitioner, as well as the therapist. Think of the empty chair or the two-chair method. Think of looking for when a symptom first appeared.

On the other hand, creative possibilities can be found when you wonder which common methods might be carried out better by the other person than by the therapist. Perhaps even purer creative possibilities can come forth when you speculate about methods that are nicely suited to being carried out by the other person, methods that do not seem to fit being 'interventions' carried out by therapists. For example, getting into a state of powerful feeling, freeing oneself of the usual controls, can be achieved when the other person spends a minute or so breathing rapidly and deeply and exhaling with powerful volume. When the other person does this, it can be useful. In contrast, few traditional therapist interventions seem to accomplish this as well as the person doing it oneself.

As another example, trying out a new way of being and behaving, here in the session, and checking to see the immediately ongoing, bodily-felt sensations, can be carried out when the person is the one who does these things. It is hard to see how therapists' interventions can do as well as the person himself in enabling the person to close his eyes, visualize his uncle standing inside the apartment, put his hands on his uncle's shoulders, say, 'Uncle Stan, you're a great guy' and then check for the accompanying bodily-felt sensations. Actually carrying out these things is probably more effectively achieved when the therapist shows the person what to do and how to do it, and the person is the one to actually carry them out, as compared with the client as the object of the therapist's usual interventions.

The main point is that you can enter the realm of creative new ideas when you enter into a creative relationship with the thing you are studying. One way of entering into a creative relationship is when, instead of your doing 'it' to the other person, the other person does it to and for oneself. I have illustrated this kind of a creative relationship, and the kinds of creative new ideas you perhaps can get, when the therapist accepts the role of teacher-guide, and the other person accepts the role of the person who carries out the methods, the role of the practitioner.

Suppose that we turn to the researcher who ordinarily studies the other person and see what creative possibilities can come to life when the researcher abandons the ordinary way of relating to the person who is the object of study and instead establishes a creative relationship with the other person. Consider a few creative possibilitie.

Picture a researcher interested in seeing whether this modification in the standard therapy gets better changes than the standard therapy itself, and the researcher had on hand ten practitioners of the standard therapy. Instead of the researcher studying the work of the ten practitioners divided into experimental and control therapists, the practitioners became integral parts of the research team itself. Suppose that there were some truly creative possibilities when the ordinary objects of study became parts of the research team itself.

One creative possibility seemed to lurk in the practitioners' suggesting that the modification be carried out by those practitioner-researchers who were indeed drawn toward the modification, rather than practitioners merely being assigned to one group or the other, or practitioners alternating between doing and not doing the modification. Sure enough, the practitioners provided evidence for their case by demonstrating that those interested in the modification did better in the training than those who were less interested.

Another creative possibility came to life when the entire research team studied the sessions and the findings, and it became clear that the practitioner-researchers were the main ones to come up with interesting and creative ideas. In short, there were some impressive ways in which some creative possibilities were opened up when the practitioners moved from being the objects of study to being integral parts of the research team itself.

Or picture a team of researchers interested in studying what it would be like to try out some explicit behaviors regarded as characteristic of people who are thought of as having attained a lofty and elevated plateau of maturity, of what human beings can become, a virtually 'optimal' level of being and behaving.

The researchers discussed what might be a relatively common design of finding subjects willing to try out these 'optimal behaviors' and to be tested and measured in regard to their progress in learning the optimal behaviors. However, a creative new direction began with one member of the research team saying that she was so drawn toward the idea of trying out these optimal behaviors that she would rather be a subject than the researcher. 'I want to try out these optimal behaviors for myself.' Most of the research team wanted to be the subjects who did the optimal behaviors rather than the researchers who studied the subjects.

Would there be some serious problems if the researchers were the ones who actually tried out the optimal behaviors? The research team put the question to a kind of test in which they actually tried out one of the optimal behaviors while a group of recruited subjects also tried carrying out the same optimal behavior. What the research team found was that they were more interested in the idea of optimal behaviors than most of the recruited subjects, they were more excitedly responsible in attending the training sessions, in actually trying out the optimal behaviors, and in doing a good job of providing the written descriptions that coinstituted the raw data of the research project. The research team did so well, and did so much better than the recruited subjects, that the research team became the subjects. They were the researchers and the research subjects.

They followed careful guidelines for carrying out the optimal behaviors and careful guidelines for describing precisely what happened when they tried out the optimal behaviors.

However, the payoff came during the regular meetings, during the long-term program of trying out the optimal behaviors, when the research team met to present the recent findings, to discuss the findings, and to assign the research tasks for the next period. These meetings were so rich in creative new ideas that the meetings alone seemed to justify researchers being both researchers and the subjects of what the researchers were studying.

It seems that there can be some creative possibilities when you fulfill the role of the teacher-guide and the other person is a practitioner, rather than the client, or the other person is the researcher-subject, rather than the subject who is studied by the researcher.

3. Become what you are studying

A creative relationship is one that fosters, opens up creative new ideas. One way of having a creative relationship is to become what you are studying.

Suppose that you are interested in studying people with attention deficit hyperactivity disorder (ADHD), depressed adolescents of depressed parents, gurus who are enlightened, incarcerated people who feel misunderstood, therapists who rely on self-disclosure, clients who have been through a corrective emotional experience in therapy, participants in mentoring relationships, or clients who are coping with cancer. How can you go about studying what you have selected to study?

The field of psychotherapy offers careful and rigorous ways of studying what you study. There are all kinds of research designs and methodologies, ways to arrive at hypotheses, ways to measure what you are to measure. You can do research. You can do clinical research. You can follow the guidelines for how to study what you are interested in studying.

You can use careful and rigorous ways of interviewing and getting data from the object of your investigation. You can ask people with ADHD to talk about it, describe it, give their impressions about it and what it is like to have the disorder. A fine interviewer can bring forth fine data about whatever the interviewer is studying.

Almost without exception, you are studying the object of your study. You are here, and the object of your study is over there. You try to be careful, rigorous and scientific in studying the object of your study. You are the researcher, the investigator, and the object of your study is what is researched, investigated.

Creative new ideas can come when you can let go of the various meanings of the role of the inquirer, the researcher, the one who seeks to know, the one who studies the other thing. Let go of seeing how it does under this and that condition. Let go of poking and probing it here and there, inspecting it, seeing how it responds and reacts to this or to that, conducting experiments on it, testing it, comparing it with other things, describing and categorizing it. Let go of any and all of the roles in which you are the one who studies it.

Instead, become that which you have studied. 'Be' it. Feel what it feels. Think what it thinks. Experience what it experiences. Be reacted and responded to the way it is reacted and responded to. Walk and talk the way it walks and talks. Sit and behave the way it sits and behaves. Your facial expressions and movements are its facial expressions and movements. Have its outlook and perception and attitude. Meld with it. Fuse with it. Be it. Join it in its being it. Undergo the radical shift from studying that person to being that person.

You are not you, living with the other person in the person's tribe or family or world. You do not have your thoughts and feelings as you walk along with the person, sit alongside the person, live with the person through the person's day and night. You are not you, swimming with the dolphins or praying with the monks or eating with the villagers in the jungle. Instead, you are joining into the other person, being the other person. You disengage wholly from being the one who studies the other person, and instead you enter wholly into being the other person, living and being as or along with the other person.

Instead of talking with the other person to try to grasp something special about that person and the person's world, you fully and completely become that person. You can know directly, rather than finding out about it from the other person. You do not try to get rid of or set aside your own way of thinking about and understanding the person. You do not try to be naive, a mere observer with your own agenda or program. You do not get simple and pure data which you then organize and put together in some ways. You do not interview the woman whose family was killed by the fellow with the bombs strapped around his waist, as he spoke in Arabic. Instead, you become her, you are her, you join with her in being her, in thinking and feeling and experiencing as she thinks and feels and experiences.

If you are competent and proficient in being the object of your study, you are the person coping with cancer. You are the person who participated in the mentoring relationship. You are the incarcerated person who feels misunderstood. You are a person with ADHD. If you are interested in studying the patient who is called psychotic, you are a patient who is called psychotic.

Suppose you are interested in studying the playful, good-humored, attractive woman who tells her colleague that his fly is open, is not zipped. If you are a male researcher, you may find yourself in the role of the male colleague, and you may have a glow of sexual embarrassment. You may take the position of a removed neutral observer who is trying to study the woman, but you will probably have a difficult time knowing what is occurring in the woman as she is saying these words to her colleague. You will probably have a difficult time knowing, even if you interview or test the woman outside the context of the immediate scene of her saying these words to her colleague. On the other hand, you may come closer to knowing when you can 'be' the woman in the immediate scene, when you can join her or be her in saying her words to her colleague.

How can you be that which you are interested in studying? How can you enter into this uncommon kind of creative relationship with the object of your study? Perhaps the main answer is for you to value this kind of creative relationship, to cherish the importance of finding better and better ways of usefully and effectively becoming what you are interested in studying. I have tried to fashion and to develop one way of accomplishing this in working with a person in experiential sessions (Mahrer, 1978, 1996/2004, 1997b; Mahrer, Boulet and Fairweather, 1994). It includes guidelines such as the following:

(a) Rather than the other person's attention being mainly on you, interacting with you, talking with you, the other person's attention is mainly on a third thing, something other than you or the other person. The third thing is to be something important, special, of significant concern or interest to the other person. For your purposes of becoming what you are studying, the more of the other person's attention is on the third thing, the better. Aim at the other person's attention being almost wholly focused on a third thing.

(b) Your attention is likewise to be mainly on the third thing. Even though your aim is to study the other person, this guideline invites you to put essentially none of your attention on the other person and as much of your attention as possible on the same third thing that the other person is mainly attending to.

(c) Position yourself so that what the person is immediately doing and saying, and how it is being done and said, are as if it is all coming from you, through you. You are the one who is doing it, saying it, and in the precise way it is being done or said. You are the vehicle. As the other person is doing or saying, you are positioned as if you are the person who is doing or saying it. You are the actor, the doer, the speaker, the one who is doing and saying what is being done and said.

Position yourself as if you are the other person, with its identity, as if you are taking up its space, being the person who is acting, doing, speaking. Think of yourself as replacing the other person, being the other person, or as melded into, joined with, fused with the other person. Think of yourself as an integral part of the other person, as if you are both inside the outer boundaries of the other person, both inside the skin of the other person. In any case, there can be new and special things happening in and to you when you are truly fused or one with what you are studying, when you are living and being with it inside its skin, when you are living and being in its immediate world along with it. You are well and truly undergoing what it can be like to be the person who is crazy, who has lost her mind, or to be the fellow who is in a state of agonized terror about the deadly cancer. However, it can be exceedingly hard to know what is new, to be able to see and describe the new things you have found, when you are sharing the identity of the other person. On the other hand, you can know what has emerged, you can see and describe what you were able to see and to undergo, when you have returned to being the observer, the outside person who can describe what happened.

What are some examples of the kinds of creative ideas you can get by being the person or thing you are interested in studying? Suppose you are with the person who is judged as being out of her mind, as being crazy, in a state of psychosis as she is transfixed by the undulating snakes on the far wall. When you withdraw out of her identity and back into being the you who is studying her, you can arrive at things because you actually went through them, things that you could probably not have found by being the observer who studies her or by interviewing her about what is occurring.

Suppose that you were simply wallowing in a particular state. There was no 'self' or 'center of awareness' that knew it was in such a state or that could report on what was occurring in here or over there with the undulating snakes on the far wall. There was no agency or 'I-ness' or 'self' who could have a conversation with an observer or researcher or interviewer. Here was an interesting, creative observation that the observer could only know first-hand when the observer detached from being the observer, melded into being the other person who was being studied, and then returned to being the observer. The creative relationship can provide you with data that you probably could not otherwise obtain.

Suppose that you are studying the person coping with the cancer. When you are being that person, when the person is attending to that cancer and saying words, you can spot the key words that are accompanied by a rising up of heightened bodily sensations. You can identify those words as 'It's going to kill me! … It doesn't care!' As these words come in and through and from both you and him, you can have access to, to sense and feel and know something that may well be outside his own awareness, something he is not quite able to report. With these words, in this immediate scene, you may have a sense of almost complicity with the merciless, uncaring, deadly, pure killing quality of the cancer. These data are available to you. You sense and undergo this quality. You have achieved this creative new idea by becoming the person with the cancer, by becoming the object of your study.

You probably have fairly standard and accepted ways of relating to what you work with and study as a teacher, supervisor, researcher and practitioner. What is more, the ways you use are probably helpful, useful, effective, and serve you well in your aims and purposes. However, if you are truly interested in entering the realm of creative new ideas, consider accepting an invitation to enter into a creative relationship with the thing you are studying, working on. The creative relationship need not replace the trusted ways you already have and use. Rather, the creative relationship is more in the spirit of something to try out when you are intent on entering the realm of creative new ideas.

A few of these creative relationships have been described in this chapter. If they are done properly, and in the right spirit, the gift can be a creative new idea.

REFERENCES

Achinstein, B (1965) Theoretical models. *British Journal for the Philosophy of Science* *16*, 102–20.

Amabile, TM (1983) *The Social Psychology of Creativity.* New York: Springer-Verlag.

Anderson, H and Goolishian, H (1992) The client is the expert: a not-knowing approach to therapy. In S McNamee and KJ Gergen (eds) *Therapy as Social Construction*, pp. 25–69. London: Sage.

Ariew, R and Barker, P (1996) Preface. *Pierre Duhem: Essays in the history and philosophy of science*, pp. vii–xx. Indianapolis: Hackett.

Barron, FX (1969) *Creative Person and Creative Process.* New York: Holt, Rinehart, and Winston.

Bartley, WW (1984) *The Retreat to Commitment.* LaSalle, IL: Open Court.

Bartley, WW (1988) Theories of rationality. In G Radnitsky and WW Bartley (eds) *Evolutionary Epistemology, Rationality, and the Sociology of Knowledge*, pp. 206–16. LaSalle, IL: Open Court.

Bolgar, H (1965) The case study method. In BB Wolman (ed) *Handbook of Clinical psychology*, pp. 28–39. New York: McGraw-Hill.

Borgen, FH (1992) Expanding scientific paradigms in counseling psychology. In SD Brown and RW Lent (eds) *Handbook of Counseling psychology*, (2nd edn), pp. 111–39. New York: Wiley.

Bridgman, PW (1928) *The Logic of Modern Physics.* New York: Macmillan.

Chalmers, AF (1982) *What is This Thing Called Science?* Queensland, Australia: University of Queensland Press.

Chubin, D and Hackett, E (1990) *Peerless Science.* Albany, NY: SUNY Press.

Csikszentmihalyi, M (1997) *Creativity: Flow and the psychology of discovery and invention.* New York: Harper Collins.

de Shazer, S (1991) *Putting Differences to Work*. New York: Norton.

Derrida, J (1978) *Writing and Difference*. Chicago: University of Chicago Press.

Duhem, P (1996) *Essays in the History and Philosophy of Science*. Indianapolis, IN: Hackett.

Edwards, DJ (1998) Types of case study work: a conceptual framework for case-based research. *Journal of Humanistic Psychology 38,* 36–70.

Einstein, A (1953) The fundamentals of theoretical physics. In H Feigl and M Brodbeck (eds) *Readings in the Philosophy of Science*, pp. 253–61. New York: Appleton-Century-Crofts.

Erwin, E (1997) *Philosophy and Psychotherapy*. London: Sage.

Feigl, H (1953) The scientific outlook: naturalism and humanism. In H Feigl and M Brodbeck (eds), *Readings in the Philosophy of Science*, pp. 8–18. New York: Appleton-Century-Crofts.

Feyerabend, PK (1972) *Against Method: Outline of an anarchistic theory of knowledge*. London: New Left Books.

Feyerabend, PK (1978) *Science in a Free Society*. London: New Left Books.

Fodor, JA (1987) *Psychosemantics: The problem of meaning in the philosophy of mind*. Cambridge, MA: MIT Press.

Follette, WC and Houte, AC (1996) Models of scientific progress, and the role of theory in taxonomy development: a case study of the DSM. *Journal of Consulting and Clinical Psychology 64,* 1120–32.

Fuller, S (1994) The sphere of critical thinking in the post-epistemic world. *Informal Logic 16,* 39–54.

Fuller, S (1996) Social epistemology and psychology. In W O'Donohue and RF Kitchener (eds) *The Philosophy of Psychology*, pp. 33–49. London: Sage.

Furnham, A (1987) *Lay Theories: Everyday understanding of problems in the social sciences*. Oxford, England: Pergamon.

Gadamer, P (1975) *Truth and Method*. New York: Seabury.

Gardner, H (1993) *Creative Minds: An anatomy of creativity seen through the lives of Freud, Einstein, Picasso, Stravinsky, Elliot, Graham, and Gandhi*. New York: Basic Books.

Gedo, JL (1997) Psychoanalytic theories of creativity. In MA Runco (ed), *The Creativity Research Handbook*, Vol. I, pp. 29–39. Cresskill, NJ: Hampton.

Giorgi, A (1986) The 'context of discovery/context of verification' distinction and descriptive human science. *Journal of Phenomenological Psychology 17,* 151–66.

Glazer, BG and Strauss, AL (1967) *The Discovery of Grounded Theory: Strategies for qualitative research*. Chicago: Aldine/Atherton.

Glover, JA, Ronning, RR and Reynolds, CR (eds) (1989) *Handbook of Creativity*. New York: Plenum.

Guilford, JP (1950) Creativity. *American Psychologist 5,* 444–54.

Hare-Mustin, RT and Maracek, J (1990) Gender and the meaning of difference: Postmodernism and psychology. In RT Hare-Mustin and J Maracek (eds) *Making a Difference: Psychology and the contribution of gender*, pp. 22–64. New Haven, CT: Yale University Press.

Henwood, KI and Pidgeon, NF (1993) Qualitative research and psychological theorizing. In M. Hammersley (ed) *Social Research: Philosophy, politics, and practice*, pp. 14–32. London: Sage.

Hocutt, M (1996) Behaviorism as opposition to Cartesianism. In W O'Donohue and RF Kitchener (eds) *The Philosophy of Psychology*, pp. 81–5. London: Sage.

Hoshmand, LT (1989) Alternate research paradigms: a review and teaching proposal. *The Counseling Psychologist 17, 3–39.*

Kagan, J (1996) Three pleasing ideas. *American Psychologist 51, 901–8.*

Kantor, JR (1945) *Psychology and Logic* (Vol. 1) Bloomington, IN: Principia.

Kantor, JR (1950) *Psychology and Logic* (Vol. 2) Bloomington, IN: Principia.

Kiesler, DJ (1994) Standardization of intervention: the tie that binds psychotherapy research and practice. In PF Talley, HH Strupp and SF Butler (eds) *Psychotherapy Research and Practice*, pp. 142–53. New York: Basic Books.

Koehler, W (1947) *Gestalt Psychology: An introduction to new concepts in modern psychology.* New York: Liveright.

Koffka, K (1935) *Principles of Gestalt Psychology.* New York: Harcourt Brace.

Kuhn, TS (1959) *The Copernican Revolution.* New York: Random House.

Kuhn, TS (1970) *The Structure of Scientific Revolutions.* Chicago: University of Chicago Press.

Kuhn. TS (1977) *The Essential Tension.* Chicago: University of Chicago Press.

Lakatos, I (1963) Proofs and refutations. *British Journal for the Philosophy of Science 14,* 1–25.

Lakatos, I (1970) Falsification and the methodology of scientific research programs. In I Lakatos and A Musgrave (eds) *Criticism and the Growth of Knowledge*, pp. 91–196. Cambridge, UK: Cambridge University Press.

Lakatos, I (1974) Popper on demarcation and induction. In PA Schilpp (ed) *The Philosophy of Karl Popper*, pp. 241–73. LaSalle, IN: Open Court.

Loar, B (1981) *Mind and Meaning.* London: Cambridge University Press.

Mach, E (1960) *The Science of Mathematics: A critical and historical account of the development,* 6th edn. LaSalle, Indiana: Open Court.

Madden, EH (1953) The philosophy of science in Gestalt theory. In H Feigl and M Brodbeck (eds) *Readings in the Philosophy of Science*, pp. 559–70. New York: Appleton-Century-Crofts.

Mahrer, AR (1978) The therapist–patient relationship: conceptual analysis and a proposal for a paradigm-shift. *Psychotherapy: Theory, Research and Practice 15, 201–15.*

Mahrer, AR (1985) *Psychotherapeutic Change: An alternative approach to meaning and measurement.* New York: Norton.

Mahrer, AR (1988) Discovery-oriented psychotherapy research: rationale, aims, and methods. *American Psychologist 43, 694–702.*

Mahrer, AR (1989) *Experiencing: A humanistic theory of psychology and psychiatry.* Ottawa, Canada: University of Ottawa Press.

Mahrer, AR (1995) An introduction to some disposable myths, how to detect them, and a short list. *Psychotherapy 32, 484–8.*

Mahrer, AR (1996a) Discovery-oriented research on how to do psychotherapy. In W Dryden (ed) *Research in Counselling and Psychotherapy: Practical applications,* pp. 232–58. London: Sage.

Mahrer, AR (1996b) Studying distinguished practitioners: a humanistic approach to discovering how to do psychotherapy. *Journal of Humanistic Psychology 36,* 31–48.

Mahrer, AR (1996/2004) *The Complete Guide to Experiential Psychotherapy.* Boulder, CO: Bull.

Mahrer, AR (1997a) What are the 'breakthrough problems' in the field of psychotherapy? *Psychotherapy 34,* 81–5.

Mahrer, AR (1997b) Empathy as therapist–client alignment. In AC Bohart and LS Greenberg (eds) *Empathy Reconsidered: New directions in psychotherapy,* pp.187–213. Washington, DC: American Psychological Association.

Mahrer, AR (1998) How can philosophy contribute to the advancement of psychotherapy? An introduction. *Clinical Psychology: Science and Practice 5,* 229–32.

Mahrer, AR (1999) Embarrassing problems for the field of psychotherapy. *Journal of Clinical Psychology 55,* 1147–56.

Mahrer, AR (2000a) What is the next big revolution in the field of psychotherapy? *Psychotherapy 37,* 354–8.

Mahrer, AR (2000b) Philosophy of science and the foundations of psychotherapy. *American Psychologist 55,* 1117–25

Mahrer, AR (2001a) Experiential psychotherapy. In RJ Corsini (ed), *Handbook of Innovative Therapy* (2nd edn), pp. 218–29. New York: Wiley.

Mahrer, AR (2001b) An historical review of the field of psychotherapy from the year 2199. *Psychotherapy Bulletin 36,* 9–14.

Mahrer, AR (2001c) An experiential alternative to countertransference. *Journal of Clinical Psychology 57,* 1021–8.

Mahrer, AR (2002a) In experiential sessions, there is no therapist or client: there is a 'teacher' and a 'practitioner'. *Journal of Contemporary Psychotherapy 32,* 71–82.

Mahrer, AR (2002b) *Becoming the Person you can Become: The complete guide to self-transformation.* Boulder, CO: Bull.

Mahrer, AR (2003) What are the foundational beliefs in the field of psychotherapy? *Psychology: Journal of the Hellenic Psychological Society 10,* 1–19.

Mahrer, AR (2004a) *Why do Research on Psychotherapy? Introduction to a revolution.* London: Whurr.

Mahrer, AR (2004b) *Theories of Truth, Models of Usefulness: Toward a revolution in the field of psychotherapy.* London: Whurr.

Mahrer, AR (2004c) Experiential psychotherapy. In RJ Corsini and D Wedding (eds), *Current Psychotherapies* (7th edn), pp. 439–74. Belmont, CA: Brooks/Cole.

Mahrer, AR (2005) *Supervision of Psychotherapists: The discovery-oriented approach.* London: Whurr.

Mahrer, AR and Boulet, DB (1999) How to do discovery-oriented psychotherapy research. *Journal of Clinical Psychology 55,* 1481–93.

Mahrer, AR, Boulet, DB and Fairweather, DR (1994) Beyond empathy: advances in the clinical theory and methods of empathy. *Clinical Psychology Review 14,* 183–98.

Mahrer, AR, Boulet, DB and Robson, J (1998) Lifelong mild bad feelings a review and a solution to a psychotherapeutic enigma. *Journal of Contemporary Psychotherapy 28,* 173–85.

Maslow. A (1971) *The Further Reaches of Human Nature.* New York: Penguin.

Mays, W (1977) *Whitehead's Philosophy of Science and Metaphysics.* The Hague, Netherlands: Martinus Nijhoff.

Millon, T (1999) *Personality-Guided Therapy*. New York: Wiley.

Nadler, G, Hibino, S and Farrell, J (1995) *Creative Solution Finding: The triumph of breakthrough thinking over conventional problem solving*. Rocklin, CA: Prima.

Paulus, P (ed) (1989) *Psychology of Group Influence* (2nd edn). Hillsdale, NJ: Lawrence Erlbaum.

Polanyi, M (1967) *Tacit Dimension*. New York: Doubleday.

Popper, KR (1972a) *Conjectures and Refutations: The growth of scientific knowledge*. New York: Harper and Row.

Popper, KR (1972b) *Objective Knowledge*. Oxford: Oxford University Press.

Popper, KR (1980) *The Logic of Scientific Discovery*. New York: Harper and Row.

Radnitsky, G (1988) In defense of self-applicable critical rationalism. In G Radnitsky and WW Hartley (eds) *Evolutionary Epistemology and the Sociology of Knowledge*, pp. 279–312. LaSalle, IL: Open Court.

Reichenbach, H (1938) *Experience and Prediction*. Chicago: University of Chicago Press.

Reichenbach, H (1953) The philosophical significance of the theory of relativity. In H Feigl and M Brodbeck (eds) *Readings in the Philosophy of Science*, pp. 195–211. New York: Appleton-Century-Crofts.

Richards, G (1996) On the necessary survival of folk psychology. In W O'Donohue and RF Kitchener (eds) *The Philosophy of Psychology*, pp. 270–75. London: Sage.

Rorty, R (1991) *Philosophy and the Mirror of Nature*. Princeton, NJ: Princeton University Press.

Rotgers, F (1988) Social learning theory, philosophy of science, and the identity of behavior therapy. In D Fishman, F Rotgers and C Franks (eds) *Paradigms in Behavior Therapy*, pp. 187–223. New York: Springer.

Schon, DA (1982) *The Reflective Practitioner: How professionals think in action*. New York: Basic Books.

Simon, HA (1996) Computational theories of cognition. In W O'Donohue and RF Kitchener (eds) *The Philosophy of Psychology*, pp. 160–72. London: Sage.

Simonton, DK (2000) Creativity: cognitive, personal, developmental, and social aspects. *American Psychologist 55*, 151–8.

Skinner, BF (1938) *The Behavior of Organisms*. New York: Appleton-Century-Crofts.

Skinner, BF (1987) Whatever happened to psychology as the science of behavior? *American Psychologist 42*, 780–6.

Slife, BD and Williams, RN (1995) *What's Behind the Research? Discovering hidden assumptions in the behavioural sciences*. London: Sage.

Stich, S (1983) *From Folk Psychology to Cognitive Science*. Cambridge, MA: MIT Press.

Taylor, E (1984) *William James on Exceptional Mental States: The 1896 Lowell Lectures*. Amherst, MA: University of Massachusetts Press.

Thorndike, EL (1932) *The Fundamentals of Learning*. New York: Columbia University Press.

Tyler, LE (1983) *Thinking Creatively* . San Francisco: Jossey-Bass.

Valentine, ER (1996) Folk psychology and its implications for cognitive science: discussion. In W O'Donohue and RF Kitchener (eds) *The Philosophy of Psychology*, pp. 275–8. London: Sage.

van Fraassen, B (1980) *The Scientific Image*. New York: Oxford University Press.

van Fraassen, B (1989) *Laws and Symmetry*. London: Oxford University Press.

Watzlawick, P, Weakland, JH and Fisch, R (1974) *Change: Principles of problem formation and problem resolution*. New York: Norton.

Weimer, WB (1979) *Notes on the Methodology of Scientific Research*. Hillsdale, NJ: Erlbaum.

Weinsheimer, JC (1985) *Gadamer's Hermeneutics: A reading of truth and method*. New Haven and London: Yale University Press.

Wertheimer, M (1944) Gestalt theory. *Social Research 11*, 78–99.

Whitehead, AN (1929) *Process and Reality: An essay in cosmology*. Cambridge: Cambridge University Press.

Winner, E (1996) *Gifted Children: Myths and realities*. New York: Basic Books.

Winner, E (2000) The origins and ends of giftedness. *American Psychologist 55*, 159–69.

NAME INDEX

SUBJECT INDEX